Parish Renewal

Parish Renewal

A Charismatic Approach

George Martin

Word of Life
Ann Arbor, Michigan

Published by: Word of Life
            P.O. Box 331
            Ann Arbor, Michigan

Printed in the United States of America

ISBN: 0-89283-030-1

Let your attitude be Christ's attitude:
His state was divine,
yet he did not cling to his equality with God
but emptied himself
to assume the condition of a slave,
and became as men are;
and being as all men are, he was humbler yet
even to accepting death,
death on a cross.

Phil 2:5-8

Contents

Preface

This book suggests attitudes and approaches to bringing charismatic renewal to the Catholic parish. It is primarily addressed to Catholics who are active in the charismatic renewal and who are concerned with establishing the proper relationship between the prayer group and the parish.

The impact of the charismatic renewal on the parish is a matter of concern for both the charismatic renewal and the Catholic Church. The challenge of parish renewal is formidable. A body of practical wisdom is needed: guidelines for relating the charismatic renewal to the parish, pitfalls to be avoided, "how-to-do-it" advice. Despite the need for such a body of wisdom, very little has so far appeared in print. This book was written as a first step toward remedying this lack. It is not offered as the last word on the subject of parish renewal. Rather, it was written in the hope that it could serve as a point of departure for groups beginning the work of parish renewal.

There are many important questions that this book does not deal with. It presumes that healthy prayer groups exist, or that advice for building them can be found elsewhere. This book does not duplicate Bert Ghezzi's *Build With the Lord*; I highly recommend his book to those seeking practical wisdom in building strong and effective prayer groups.

This book does not attempt to discuss all the efforts at parish renewal going on in the Catholic Church today.

Its focus is limited to the charismatic renewal and its particular impact on parish life. This does not mean that the charismatic movement has a monopoly on parish renewal, or that these other efforts at renewal are without value.

Neither do I deal with a number of important questions emerging in the charismatic renewal. How should ecumenical prayer groups relate to the Catholic parish (or to local Protestant churches)? How can the sacraments be renewed in the power of the Spirit? Should Christians be immersed in the world as a leaven, or withdrawn from it as a counter-culture and sign? How is the Vatican Council's goal of an ecumenically united Body of Christ to be achieved? These are all important questions, and some of them bear on the charismatic renewal of parish life. But their importance and complexity puts them beyond the scope of this modest book.

We are only beginning to learn how the charismatic renewal may be successfully integrated into parish life and bring renewal to the parish. Few successful experiences have been described in writing; the outstanding exception is *In God's Providence,* Fr. John Randall's book about the renewal of St. Patrick's parish in Providence, Rhode Island. It would be desirable to gather together a great variety of experiences, from small parishes and large, from urban and rural settings, from all-Catholic and Catholic-ecumenical prayer groups, and discuss them as various models for charismatic parish renewal. Such a book is in the planning stage, and would serve as a complementary volume to this present book.

The suggestions of many people have been helpful in shaping this book—particularly of members of the Advisory Committee to the Catholic Charismatic Renewal Service Committee; the priests of Bethany House of Intercession in Rhode Island; the coordinators of the New Orleans' Pastoral Team; Fr. John Randall of St. Patrick's, Providence, Rhode Island; and the editors of Word of Life. Final responsibility for the adequacy or inadequacy of the advice offered here must rest with the author, however.

George Martin
February 1, 1976

1

The Current Situation

The goal of the charismatic renewal within the Catholic Church is a charismatically renewed Catholic Church. The ultimate aim is not to have a successful and thriving Catholic charismatic movement, but to have a complete renewal of Christian life in the power of the Spirit. The charismatic renewal is in the Church and for the Church. Its purpose is the renewal of the Church.

If these are basic principles to guide the charismatic renewal today, we must apply them to parish life. To relate properly to the Church as a whole, the charismatic renewal must establish a correct relationship to the local parish, and bring renewal to the parish. The charismatic renewal will not have its full impact on the Church unless it plays a role in parish renewal.

For the vast majority of Catholics today, Church life is synonymous with parish life. The parish is the point of contact between the Catholic and his Church. It is the normal context in which the Catholic lives out his Christian life; it is his primary source of Christian fellowship; it is the single most important source for the teaching that guides him; it is the place where he joins with others in worship and the celebration of the sacraments.

To be a Catholic means to be a member of a specific parish. Parish membership is not a matter of choice— not even the choice of which parish one belongs to. With rare exceptions, parish membership is determined geographically, on the basis of where one lives. The Catholic parish is the most local unit of the universal Church. A fundamental part of the "pastoral strategy" of the Catholic Church is this geographic or territorial division of the Church into smaller units for pastoral care and teaching, for common worship, and for the celebration of the sacraments.

Because the basic pastoral structure of the Church is made up of the geographic communities we call parishes, the charismatic renewal must come to grips with parish life if the Catholic Church is to be charismatically renewed. Non-geographic structures and institutions such as religious orders, universities, and even "free-floating" parishes are important parts of the Church's life, and sometimes have powerful effects on the lives of Catholics. But the basic organizational pattern and pastoral approach of the Church is the geographic parish. A movement that becomes incarnated in local parish life has the best chance of effecting a major and lasting renewal.

This point needs emphasis. The Church is based on geographically determined local communities. A fundamental renewal of the Church must involve a renewal of the basic building blocks of Church life—geographic parishes.

Most observers of parish life agree that parishes need renewal. Far too many parishes offer only a minimal amount of pastoral care to their members; far too many lack any discernible vitality; far too many are communities in name only. The Church's pastoral structure is not perfect, nor is its pastoral strategy working flawlessly.

Some have even wondered whether the current parish structure has a future. Even bishops have admitted that parish priests alone do not have the time and resources to adequately care for the thousands of Catholics who make up our large parishes. The past decade has seen numerous attempts to create new forms of parish life. Perhaps the best-known efforts at structural renewal have involved "free-floating" experimental parishes whose membership is not limited to Catholics from one geographic area. While non-geographic parishes and other structural forms have been widely publicized, their successes have been modest. They do not appear to be a replacement for geographic parishes.

Parish structure may well evolve over the next few years, but the evolution will come slowly. It would be a mistake for charismatic prayer groups to avoid relating to the parish structure today on the grounds that new structures will replace geographic parishes. It is better to come to grips with existing parish structure today, without excessive theoretical speculations about the likely pattern of parish life tomorrow. It will be easier to relate to the parish tomorrow if a proper relationship has been established with the parish today.

When we look at the Catholic charismatic renewal today, we are first of all struck by its diversity and complexity. Some prayer groups are very small, with less than a dozen participants. Some are very large, with over 1,000 members. Some groups have only the loosest of ties among members, and really exist only during their weekly gatherings. Other groups have evolved into tightly knit communities, with their members committing their entire lives to each other. Some groups are exclusively made up of Roman Catholics. Other groups are to varying degrees ecumenical in their membership.

Nevertheless, many Catholic prayer groups can in some sense be termed "parish prayer groups": either made up heavily of people from one parish, or focusing their activities in one parish. But even here there is much diversity. In several cases, full "charismatic parishes" where all or most of a parish becomes identified with the charismatic renewal are beginning to emerge. The best-known example of a charismatic parish is St. Patrick's in Providence, Rhode Island. At the other extreme are smaller groups, with members drawn from one parish, meeting in the parish hall with the benign (but distant) approval of the pastor, but having little impact on parish life.

Such parish prayer groups may well constitute a majority of groups in the Catholic charismatic renewal. About half the groups listed in the 1975-76 Directory of Catholic charismatic prayer groups have fewer than 25 members; three-fourths of them have less than 50 members. Similarly, almost half the groups listed are completely Catholic in their makeup, and about three-fourths of them are more than 80 percent Catholic. Roughly one group in every three is made up entirely of Catholics and has fewer than 25 members. Many groups, particularly small ones, meet in private homes. However, almost half of all prayer groups listed meet on parish property— church, school, parish hall, or rectory.

Thus, while there is considerable diversity in the Catholic charismatic renewal, the most common pattern is one of small groups, entirely or heavily made up of Catholics, meeting somewhere in the parish on a weekly basis.

The pastoral strategies of the charismatic renewal are as diverse as the structure and composition of prayer groups. The movement is not evolving in a single direction. Some prayer groups are forming themselves into covenant communities. But most prayer groups are not attempting to form communities, and should not be encouraged to do so: the formation of a community is no easy task. Other groups are looser associations of individuals whose strongest commitment is to the parish. Some groups are trying to evolve a truly ecumenical style of life, while respecting the denominational affiliations of their members. Other groups are firmly committed to being exclusively Roman Catholic in their orientation and membership.

In general, the Catholic charismatic renewal today is neither fully integrated into parish life nor has it formed itself into a permanently separate structure. On the whole, the movement usually has some kind of ties to a local parish, but has yet had only limited impact on parish life. Most groups are searching for the right kind of relationship to their parish and are anxious to come under the right kind of pastoral direction from their pastor. And there is a good deal of uncertainty on all sides how this is to be accomplished.

Some large, city-wide prayer groups have divided themselves into smaller, parish-based groups in order to have more impact on parishes—and found that they did not have the resources to sustain the smaller groups. Such a change meant that a limited number of leaders gifted with pastoral skills had to spread themselves too thinly over too many small groups. Sometimes a certain "critical mass" of individuals with charismatic gifts is necessary to sustain a group; the division of a large, vibrant prayer group into smaller groups may result in a general loss of intensity and life in all the prayer groups involved.

Some parish-based prayer groups have attempted parish renewal—and failed spectacularly. Many individuals have attempted to spark a charismatic renewal of their parishes—only to become frustrated at their lack of success and to eventually abandon their efforts. Some would go so far as to say that parish renewal is an impossible ideal, and that the only hope for the Church lies in creating new structures of communal life.

At best, parish renewal is never easy. Not every prayer group should undertake it as a primary mission. To determine whether a group should make a major effort in parish renewal, its leaders and members should examine three factors with special care: the internal strength of the group, the composition of the group, and the situation of the parish in question.

Some prayer groups should not attempt parish renewal because they are internally weak. These are groups which are struggling with such unresolved problems as poorly defined or unacknowledged leadership, an inadequate program of teaching, and an absence of important spiritual gifts. Very small groups and groups with uncertain membership and widely fluctuating attendance at the weekly prayer meeting should proceed cautiously in the direction of parish renewal.

Other groups should proceed cautiously because of the composition of their membership. Some large and effective prayer groups are composed of people from many different parishes in a city or region. To concentrate resources on one parish to the neglect of others may involve decisions and commitments that many members of the prayer group cannot share. In addition, ecumenical prayer groups risk driving their Protestant members away if they make renewal of a Catholic parish their exclusive concern. Ecumenical fellowship and parish renewal are both aspects of the Lord's work in the charismatic renewal. Balancing them in a local prayer group calls for the utmost sensitivity, tact, and attentiveness to the Lord's will.

Finally, some parishes are not receptive to charismatic renewal. If the pastor is openly or even subtly hostile to the prayer group, it may well be impossible for charismatic renewal of the parish to even begin. (We shall discuss the role of the pastor more fully in Chapter 5.)

Nonetheless, renewal of parish life in the power of the Spirit must be an area of high concern for the charismatic renewal. If the charismatic renewal exists for the renewal of the Church, the necessity of parish renewal cannot be ignored.

An obvious first step toward bringing the charismatic renewal to the parish is to develop prayer groups within parishes that do not have them. Although this may be an obvious step, it is not necessarily the correct one, or the first one. Guidelines developed by Benny Suhor for use in the Archdiocese of New Orleans recommend a cautious, step-by-step approach in starting a charismatic prayer group in a parish. These guidelines, aimed at people who wish to start a parish charismatic prayer group, include the following points:

1. Place everything in the hands of the Lord. "Unless the Lord build the house, they labor in vain who build it" (Ps. 127:1).
2. Start attending prayer meetings on a regular weekly basis at one of the larger prayer groups in your area.
3. Take the Life in the Spirit Seminar and be prayed over for a deeper life in the Holy Spirit ("baptized in the Holy Spirit").
4. Continue to attend a large prayer meeting weekly, but meet at another time during the week with other members of your parish who have followed the same steps. With them, praise the Lord and ask him to guide you in your work in the parish.

   In most cases, it is better to have these small prayer meetings in your homes rather than in one of the parish buildings. Also, it is usually better not to invite non-charismatic friends to these meetings.
5. You are probably ready to be recognized as a *parish* charismatic prayer group when the following situations have come about:
   a) A dozen or more parishioners have been meeting regularly to pray in the small groups and are mature enough in the charismatic gifts to sustain a charismatic prayer meeting at which other parishioners would be present.
   b) There is real *leadership* to sustain such a charismatic prayer group. If you feel you must

invite an outsider to come lead your prayer meetings, you are probably not ready to be recognized publicly as a *parish* charismatic prayer group. When the Lord wants you to be a bona fide *parish* charismatic prayer group, he will give you the leadership from within your own parish.

If this leadership does not seem to emerge within your small group, just continue to meet in one another's homes, asking the Lord to raise up leaders among you. If a small group like this does not have leadership, it can hardly expect to exercise leadership when it begins to operate on a larger scale when other parishioners start to attend.

c) Your pastor is willing to give you support, encouragement, and the use of a parish facility for your prayer meetings.

d) There is adequate male leadership for the group. In general, men tend to avoid involvement in prayer groups that are led by women. Some prayer groups, such as daytime prayer groups, will be composed of women and led by women. But a prayer group which wants to function as a parish prayer group, open to all parishioners, should have adequate male leadership.

6. Resist the temptation to do too much too soon with too many people. Be patient. Recall Jesus' words to his apostles: "*Wait*, rather, for the fulfillment of my Father's promise" (Acts 1:4). And note what they did during this time of waiting: "They went to the upstairs room. Together they devoted themselves to constant prayer" (Acts 1:13-14).

Our parishes will be renewed in the Lord's time, not ours. He wants a deep renewal in his people. He does not want a spiritual "flash in the pan."

Above all, focus on Jesus, not on success. "Unless the Lord build the house, they labor in vain who build it."

One point in these guidelines deserves emphasis. Above all, the Lord must lead the development of a parish prayer group. The people who form the core of the prayer group should continually seek the Lord's guidance. The Lord will set the timing for the prayer group and for parish renewal. Those who have responsibility for this work must listen to the Lord, wait for him to speak, and act when they hear his voice. The task of receiving the Lord's guidance is not magical, but rather calls forth all our powers of study, analysis, patience, and prayer. It is nevertheless essential. Without the Lord's guidance, all attempts at renewal—parish or otherwise—are doomed to failure. (We will discuss guidance more fully in Chapter 4.)

It would also be well to stress the importance of a prayer group, rather than an isolated individual, undertaking the work of parish renewal. In some cases, individuals have left city-wide prayer groups to go back to their parishes to "get something started." Often the challenge of parish renewal can overwhelm the lone individual. It would be better to maintain membership in a regional prayer group for support, until such time as a viable parish prayer group has been established.

A word also needs to be said about the basic perspective of the charismatic renewal toward parish renewal.

Charismatic renewal and parish renewal are not synonymous. The charismatic renewal is not the only way the Spirit is renewing parish life, and parish renewal is only one of the works the Lord is accomplishing through the charismatic renewal.

On the one hand, parishes have changed and will continue to change because of numerous movements and innovations which have emerged since the Second Vatican Council. The charismatic renewal is only one of these movements. Some of these changes are aimed at helping the Church carry out its mission with more efficiency—for example, by drawing on the insights of management science to help develop diocesan pastoral plans. Other changes have more to do with the Church's inner life, and are aimed at fostering spiritual renewal. The Liturgical Movement is one example of such a movement.

Hence, despite the importance of the charismatic renewal, it is not the only way the Spirit is moving to renew the Church. The typical parish today is experiencing various kinds of renewal; it is not simply standing idle, waiting for the charismatic renewal to meet its needs.

At the same time, the charismatic renewal is not simply a means for parish renewal. Many solid and desirable developments from the charismatic renewal cannot simply and easily be made part of the parish structure as we know it. For example, the charismatic renewal is providing the basis for more solidly grounded ecumenical fellowship between Catholics and Protestants than anywhere else in the Church today. It is difficult to see how this ecumenical fellowship could be completely subsumed into the parish structure. The bonds of commitment being forged in covenant communities are an impressive witness to the presence of the Spirit. It is not clear how such communities should relate to the parish, particularly when they draw Catholics from a number of different parishes.

We thus need to avoid two errors: the error of identifying charismatic renewal and parish renewal too closely, and the opposite error of separating charismatic and parish renewal too rigidly. Parish renewal should be one of the prime thrusts of the charismatic renewal in the Catholic Church. What happens in the local parish will to a very large extent determine the future of the charismatic renewal—and the future of the Church. Parish renewal should be a matter of very high concern for many of the groups that make up the Catholic charismatic renewal today. This book is written primarily for members of these groups—groups which have the resources and opportunities to contribute to parish renewal.

The advice given in this book must be applied with discernment. The great diversity among parishes and among prayer groups makes any generalizations risky. It is important for us to examine *our* parish and *our* prayer group without our view being clouded by "national averages" or "current trends." A book such as this one can only deal with the general picture—but each of us as an individual is a member of a *specific* parish and *specific* prayer group. We must respond to the call of the Lord for us, in our *specific* situation.

2

Integration and Renewal

If the goal of a charismatically renewed Catholic Church is to be achieved, two basic challenges face prayer groups: the *integration* of the charismatic renewal into parish life, and the *renewal* of parish life in the power of the Spirit. It is not enough for prayer groups to function well, constantly introducing new people into a fuller life in the Spirit. It is not enough for spiritual gifts to be freely exercised in prayer meetings. The goal of a charismatically renewed Catholic Church demands that the charismatic renewal become integrated into the life of the parish and bring renewal to the parish.

Integration

The charismatic renewal will not be integrated into the Church automatically. Indeed, it conceivably might never happen at all. Prayer groups could remain separate groupings within the Church, a type of special interest club. A charismatic prayer meeting could be viewed as a "department of spiritual experiences" for a parish, a gathering of people "who go in for that sort of thing." A citywide prayer community could remain a place where Catholics from many parishes go to supplement their normal parish life. Their normal parish life would continue as usual: participation in the charismatic renewal would be something "added on" to the "essentials" of being a Catholic.

If this were to happen, the charismatic renewal would fall far short of renewing the Church. Those individuals who became a part of a prayer group would receive personal help—but the charismatic renewal as a whole would have little impact on the parish. Every parish could have its pentecostal prayer group, sharing parish facilities along with the Altar Society, the Dad's Club, the Fatima Guild, and so on. The charismatic renewal would have become an accepted part of parish life—in the sense of becoming an optional activity along with many others.

The above is an accurate description of the current status of prayer groups in many parishes. In one sense, acceptance of the charismatic renewal as a special grouping within the parish may be a mark of success. In some parishes, such acceptance has been difficult to achieve. But in another sense, such acceptance is dangerously incomplete. It is not enough for the charismatic renewal to gain acceptance as a special club—if such acceptance implies that the charismatic renewal has relevance for only one segment of the parish. In the same way, it is not enough for the charismatic renewal to be approved as one more organization within the Church, if such approval does not look to the eventual full integration of the charismatic renewal into the life of the Church.

There are many specialized groups within the Church

today. Yet even those movements which involve hundreds of thousands of Catholics—the Christian Family Movement, the Cursillo, Marriage Encounters, and others—generally have only a limited impact on the life of the Church. They exist as specialized groupings within the Church, or carry out their activities outside the mainstream of Church life. Despite their inner vitality and the large numbers of people involved in them, these movements generally have not made a difference in the life of the Church as a whole. This does not mean that these movements are failures, or are not making any contribution to the Church. The point is that they have not become fully integrated into the life of the Church.

Many of these movements thrive or fail independently of parish life. A CFM group can be effectively active in local politics, but the rest of the parish could be uninformed of its activity and uninvolved in it. Marriage Encounters could be renewing individual marriages while the rest of the life of the parish slowly slips into disrepair. Or on the other hand, there could be a very dynamic parish that lacks any of these specialized groupings within it.

I am not concerned here to judge the validity of the various movements existing within the Church today. My point is simply that most of these movements, whatever their merits, are not fully integrated into the life of the Church. If the charismatic renewal is called to become completely integrated into the Church, then it will have to follow a path different from many other movements and organizations within the Church. If the ultimate goal is one of integration, then the charismatic renewal cannot indefinitely remain a specialized grouping.

It must someday become so absorbed into the life of the Church that it is indistinguishable from it; it must someday be so much a part of the Church that it has an impact on the life of every Catholic.

This does not mean that someday every Catholic will consider himself a part of "the Catholic charismatic renewal movement." Even if every Catholic were someday to so identify himself, this would not necessarily mean that the charismatic renewal had been integrated into the life of the Church, or that it would have the kind of impact it should. Conceivably, every Catholic married couple could attend a Cursillo and a Marriage Encounter and join CFM—but neither would this mean that these movements were integrated into the life of the Church. Parish life could continue pretty much as usual, despite the success of these movements in involving large numbers of people.

I personally doubt that there will ever come a time when every Catholic will consider himself a member of the "Catholic pentecostal movement." I hope that every Catholic will live out in the fullest way possible the life of the Spirit that he received in baptism into Jesus Christ. But—and this is a different matter—I have little hope that every Catholic will someday join the special movement that the Catholic charismatic renewal currently is.

Perhaps an example will illustrate this point. Sometimes a person involved in the charismatic renewal will ask me, "Is Joe Spirit-filled?" I usually find this an awkward question, and have to answer something like this: "To the best of my knowledge, Joe is a very devout Catholic, dedicated to God, who received the Holy Spirit when he was baptized. In that sense, he is 'Spirit-filled.' But he is not involved in the charismatic renewal, does not attend prayer meetings and does not exhibit those spiritual gifts and forms of prayer that are usually associated with the charismatic renewal." My reply usually disappoints the questioner, who was looking for a simple yes or no answer. But I think the distinction is important: living the life of the Spirit cannot be limited to engaging in characteristically pentecostal forms of prayer and piety.

The goal of the charismatic renewal should be that everyone be truly "Spirit-filled": living the life of the Spirit as fully and freely as possible. The goal is not that every Christian adopt certain forms of prayer and behavior, or exercise certain spiritual gifts, or speak of their relationship with God with a certain terminology. Being a "Spirit-filled Christian" cannot be equated with simply attending charismatic prayer meetings. The ultimate aim of the charismatic renewal is not merely to build bigger and better prayer meetings, but to foster everyone's growth in the life of the Spirit.

Thus the integration of the charismatic renewal into the Church does not mean that someday every Catholic will identify himself as a "Catholic pentecostal" and attend special meetings of the "Catholic pentecostal movement." Integration means just the opposite: it means that ultimately the charismatic renewal will become so much a part of the normal life of the Church that it will no longer exist as a separate movement.

We therefore look forward to the day when the charismatic renewal will be integrated into the "mainstream" of Church life: the life which every member of the Church shares, regardless of whether he is a member of any special grouping within the Church. The "mainstream" of Church life is what one experiences by being a member of a parish, attending Sunday mass, and shaping one's life in accordance with the teachings of the Church. When a movement has become fully integrated into the life of the Church, it has an impact on this "mainstream" of life. By contrast, a specialized movement within the Church is one that has an impact primarily on those who are members of that movement. A movement that has become integrated into the mainstream of Church life has an impact on all members of the Church, simply because they are members of the Church and participate in the life of the Church.

Some movements have achieved such successful integration. At one time there was an identifiable Liturgical Movement within the Catholic Church: a group of people consciously working to improve the Church's worship. The Liturgical Movement had its identifiable leaders and spokesmen, its own distinctive publications, its own conferences, its own special aims, even its own distinctive terminology. Most of the Liturgical Movement's aims to change the Church's forms of worship have been accomplished, and today the Liturgical Movement no longer exists as a separate movement in the same way it once did. Before Vatican II, those who thought the liturgy should be in the vernacular went to special meetings to discuss it. Now they attend Sunday mass in English, along with every other Catholic in English-speaking countries. Because it accomplished its goals, the Liturgical Movement has had an impact on every Catholic's worship.

The Liturgical Movement achieved integration into

the life of the Church chiefly through decisions made by the bishops of the Church at the Second Vatican Council. The Liturgical Movement prepared the way for these liturgical changes. The Liturgical Movement was a prophetic movement, pointing out how an essential element of the Church's life needed to be renewed. The charismatic renewal stands in a similar relationship to the Church today.

There has also been what might be called a "Biblical Movement" going on in the Church for some years. Although the Biblical Movement was generally less organized and less clearly identifiable than the Liturgical Movement, it too has had its particular goals and a corresponding impact on the life of the Church. Based on the work of scholars who wanted to understand Scripture better and to help Catholics read Scripture as the word of God, the Biblical Movement has influenced how the Catholic Church as a whole uses Scripture in many aspects of its life.

The goal of the Biblical Movement has not been to create a group of specialist Bible readers in the Church, but it has instead aimed at making every dimension of the Church's life more scripturally oriented. As a result of the movement, far better translations of Scripture are available to Catholics today than there were 20 years ago. These translations are apparently being more widely read, and are leading to a fuller and more widespread understanding of God's word. Religious education programs and textbooks have been revised to be more scripturally based, and to proclaim more clearly the saving truth that Jesus is Lord. Many songs based on Scripture have been composed, and are now in common use in the

Church. Following the directives of Vatican II, preachers are giving more attention to Scripture: scripturally-based "homilies" have generally displaced the standard Sunday "sermon" that was once a fixture at mass. The whole tone of the liturgy has become much more scriptural.

Catholics have been so influenced in so many areas by the Biblical Movement that it can truly be said to have entered into the mainstream of the Church. Yet there is no special club of "Bible promoters" in each parish. The Biblical Movement has not so much formed a special movement of Bible devotees as much as permeated the whole life of the Church with Scripture. The Biblical Movement is so integrated into the life of the Church today that it can scarcely be identified as a separate movement.

Such integration into the life of the Church is the ultimate call of the charismatic renewal. For the time being, a charismatic renewal movement is needed in the Catholic Church. For the time being, a group of people must explore the full meaning of the presence of the Spirit in the Church, develop wisdom about the use of charismatic gifts, experiment in new forms of community life and prayer, and bring a fuller meaning of life in the Spirit to the Catholic Church. But the ultimate aim of the charismatic renewal is to bring about a renewal of the Church. Its goal is not to perpetuate itself as a special movement. To accomplish its ultimate goal, the charismatic renewal cannot exist indefinitely as a specialized grouping; it must ultimately disappear into the Church, as leaven into dough.

Renewal

The charismatic renewal is not called to dissolve into the life of the Church by simply ceasing to be. It is called to make some important and specific changes in how the Church lives its life and carries out its mission.

Few would argue today that the Catholic Church does not stand in need of renewal. The Second Vatican Council was expected to spark a renewal: a fresh focus on the essentials of Christianity, a vigorous rededication to carrying out the mission of the Church, an effective presence of the Church in the modern world. During and immediately after Vatican II, many Catholics were eager to follow the Council's vision, and the promise of quick and easy renewal produced a sense of euphoria. When actual renewal was found to be slow and difficult to achieve, euphoria gave way to discouragement and disillusionment. Changes were made—but they often failed to bring the expected results. Parish councils were created—but parishes were not thereby transformed overnight into vibrant Christian communities. Polarizations occurred between those who thought renewal was moving too slowly and those who thought change was occurring too rapidly.

Much of this tension and disillusionment has diminished in recent years. There seems to be less hope among Catholics for a rapid renewal of the Church, and correspondingly less discouragement when renewal does indeed come slowly. But if the extremes of hope and discouragement have diminished, the Church's need for renewal has not. Much of the Council's vision for renewal has yet to be fulfilled.

Many aspects of Church life are showing signs of deterioration. Attendance at Sunday mass has declined: now only slightly more than 50 percent of those who identify themselves as Catholic regularly attend Sunday mass—a decline from the more than 70 percent who regularly attended 20 years ago. Adult converts to Catholicism have steadily dwindled year by year, and are now only a trickle. Vocations to the priesthood and religious life have dropped markedly.

These statistics tell only a part of the story. Declining numbers would be less alarming if at the same time the quality of Christian life in the Catholic Church was markedly improving. But it is apparently not. Few parishes appear to be the kind of dynamic Christian communities they are called to be. Some pastors seem to have been reduced to a grim holding operation style of ministry: they try faithfully and courageously to preserve as much parish life as they can, but lack long-range hope for making significant improvements.

The current challenge should not be exaggerated: the Catholic Church is not going to disappear overnight. No downward trend is so pronounced that doom certainly lies ahead. And there are positive trends; signs of hope. The Liturgical and Biblical Movements have contributed to the vitality of the Church. If parish councils have not fulfilled the extravagant hopes that they initially aroused, they have still made a positive contribution to parish life. The Catholic Church shows no signs of being swept away in an avalanche of social change—but it does show signs of erosion in many areas. And it certainly stands in need of renewal if it is to be the unblemished bride of Christ that it is called to be.

In particular, the Church needs greater spiritual vitality and pastoral effectiveness. It needs greater power in calling men to repentance and faith in Jesus Christ, greater effectiveness in helping its members mature in the Christian life, an increased ability to knit Christians' lives together in various forms of community. The Church needs the variety of ministry gifts that are helpful in carrying out its pastoral mission. Its overriding need is for an increased vitality of Christian life, so that the Body of Christ may be built up and be an effective witness to Christ in the world today.

The charismatic renewal has much to offer the Church in its current condition. Some of its contributions can be considered "charismatic" in a specialized sense, but many others are truths which the Church has long held and which are constantly in need of renewal. For example, the charismatic renewal stresses a clear focus on the evangelical proclamation of the good news about Jesus Christ; it reminds us that continued growth in the Christian life is essential; it includes a growing awareness of the importance of relationships among Christians in various forms of common life. These aspects of renewal will be explored more fully in a later chapter. For now, it is enough to focus on the more "charismatic" dimensions of the charismatic renewal.

One important dimension of the charismatic renewal is a renewal in the exercise of spiritual gifts or charisms. These gifts are given for the building up of the Body of Christ, for equipping it to carry out its mission, for enabling it to live its life. The Lord does not give the spiritual gifts merely to build better prayer meetings; he gives them so that the Church might work with greater power and effectiveness. The charismatic gifts can meet many of the Church's needs today. The charisms bring power to the proclamation of the Christian message. They provide guidance in making decisions and discerning God's will. They equip men for the variety of ministries needed to nourish the Christian community's life and to carry out the Church's mission.

Charisms are not gifts to the charismatic renewal; they are gifts to the Church. They are meant to have an impact on the life of the Church, and they must play a role in renewing the spiritual vitality of the Church.

The charismatic renewal is both a means of bringing renewal to the Church, and a sign that the Church stands in need of renewal. The very success of the charismatic renewal indicates that something has been largely missing in the Church's life—something that people are turning to the charismatic renewal to find.

No one should have to seek out a special group or meeting to receive help in entering into a fuller life of the Spirit; the availability of such help should be the characteristic of any gathering of Christians. No one should have to attend special "prayer meetings" in order to exercise spontaneous praise; such praise should have its proper place in the Church's liturgy. We should expect to hear inspired preaching and teaching from every pulpit. We should expect physical healing from the Sacrament of the Anointing of the Sick. We should expect to receive prophetic guidance and exhortation during Sunday mass.

I am not claiming that these elements are totally missing from the Church's normal life right now. Nor will I claim that the charismatic renewal has a monopoly on the gifts and graces of the Spirit. But I do believe that the charismatic renewal is called to bring about changes in how the Church lives its life. The rapid growth of the charismatic renewal is a sign that many Catholics have a spiritual hunger that is not being nourished in their normal parish life. I believe that it is a tragedy that it is not. I look forward to the day when the normal life of every Catholic parish is such that no one will need to become a "Catholic charismatic"—because the normal life of their parish will contain all those elements that they now seek out in charismatic prayer meetings.

The charismatic renewal of the Church will not happen by parishes simply adopting "pentecostal" practices on a wholesale basis. Not every custom or practice now common in the charismatic renewal should be adopted into the life of the Church. A winnowing process is needed to sort out the renewal that the Spirit is offering the Church from the cultural forms they are sometimes expressed in. For example, whether everyone should be encouraged to raise their arms when they pray is a matter for pastoral discernment. Praying with uplifted arms can be a freeing experience—or it could be a divisive practice, bringing disunity to a parish. The judgment is a pastoral one. The Church will continue to be pluralistic in its forms of life, while united in its faith in one Lord. There is room in the Church for many differences in approach and practice, as long as our unity in Jesus Christ joins us together.

The charismatic renewal is called both to bring new forms of life to the Church and to bring increased vitality to many of its existing forms. The sacraments can be celebrated with a renewed meaning and impact; existing forms of worship can take on a new vitality. But charismatic activity should not be restricted to the sacraments, nor always be made to fit into present worship forms. Laymen as well as priests should pray for the healing of the sick. Sunday liturgies should not be the only times that Catholics gather together to worship the Lord. There is room and need for many kinds of small groupings of Christians within established parishes.

When prophecy becomes an expected part of Sunday liturgies, it will not mean that prophecy is unneeded the rest of the week. It will mean, however, that prophecy has become a gift for the entire parish, not only for one segment of the parish. The integration of the charismatic renewal into the Church will not mean that "charismatic prayer meetings" will disappear; it will mean that a charismatic element will permeate every dimension of the Church's life. St. Paul was not writing about "prayer meetings" in 1 Corinthians 11-14; he was writing about the liturgy of the Church. The various kinds of charismatic activities now going on should not be an alternative to normal parish life; they should be an integrated part of parish life.

The aim of the charismatic renewal is a transformation of the life of the Church by the power of the Holy Spirit. The goal of the charismatic renewal is a Church so charismatically renewed and alive that a separate charismatic movement is entirely unneeded.

3

Seeking Unity

There are a number of challenges which will have to be met if the charismatic renewal is to become integrated into the Church and bring renewal to it. This chapter will focus on only one of these challenges—but one of the most important. This is the challenge of unity. The charismatic renewal is called to seek, preserve, and foster unity within the Body of Christ. Unity must be a standard guiding the charismatic renewal along every step of its way.

During the Last Supper, Jesus prayed that his followers would be so one in heart and mind that their unity would be a sign of his divinity. "May they all be one, Father, may they be one in us, as you are in me and I am in you, so that the world may believe it was you who sent me" (John 17:21). The unity of Christians is to be a witness of their call; it is to be a sign of the presence of the Holy Spirit in their midst.

St. Paul likewise placed the highest priority on the unity of Christians. "If our life in Christ means anything to you, if love can persuade at all, or the Spirit that we have in common, or any tenderness of sympathy, then be united in your convictions and united in your love, with a common purpose and a common mind. That is the one thing which would make me completely happy'' (Phil. 2:1-2). In his epistles, Paul's advice and his solutions to problems very frequently aim at fostering unity in the Body of Christ. He urges Christians to adopt attitudes and take actions which avoid disunity and nourish unity: ''There must be no competition among you, no conceit; but everybody is to be self-effacing. Always consider the other person to be better than yourself, so that nobody thinks of his own interests first but everybody thinks of other people's interests instead'' (Phil. 2:3-4).

Unity is a concern for all Christians, but it is a special challenge for Christians involved in movements of renewal. Throughout Church history, we can note a tendency for tension to occur between Christians involved in renewal movements and those who are not. Our concern here is not so much to discuss disunity in the larger Church as to examine division in parishes resulting from the charismatic renewal.

First, we must face the reality of such disunity and deal with it. Disunity is not a problem for every parish or charismatic prayer group. But where disunity exists in any local situation, we should acknowledge it and take steps to repair it. We cannot overcome problems of disunity if we pretend that they do not exist. Nor should we simply assume that a sovereign act of God will resolve such problems. God does act to bring the Church to unity—but he usually chooses to act through human effort. Our own understanding of the pitfalls of disunity can only help bring about the renewal that God wishes to bring to the Church.

Disunity occurs in different forms and stems from different causes. Here we shall focus on the two chief types of disunity that can occur within a parish being influenced by the charismatic renewal: the alienation of charismatically involved Catholics from the parish, and division within the parish over the charismatic renewal.

Alienation

Some degree of alienation has taken place when Catholics involved in the charismatic renewal feel less a part of their parish, when they feel less welcome and at home there, and when they become less involved in worthwhile parish activities. At its extreme, alienation can result in Catholics leaving the Church—although fortunately this rarely happens. But to the extent that involvement in the charismatic renewal is associated with a low degree of involvement in the life of the parish, alienation is taking place, and is a matter of concern.

Some of the causes for the alienation of charismatic Catholics from the Church are superficial matters of style and emphasis. For example, the style of worship that the charismatic renewal finds most congenial is different from the style of worship of most parishes. A Sunday mass performed mechanically can seem dead when compared to a lively prayer meeting. We can fall into a temptation to make prayer meetings the focus of our spiritual life, because more "seems to happen" at prayer meetings.

Other reasons for alienation go deeper and act more subtly. Catholics who have never received any instruction about how to read Scripture as the Word of God can fall into an unbiblical fundamentalism when they first discover on a personal level that Scripture is indeed God's word to us. Sometimes this can result from the influence of fundamentalist teaching. More often it results from the lack of any sound teaching on how to go about reading Scripture—a situation for which both the charismatic renewal and the Catholic Church must share the blame. Catholic charismatics rarely hold fundamentalism as an explicit intellectual position; more frequently, they fall into this error unconsciously, for the lack of sound guidance. But fundamentalism can play a contributing role in alienating charismatics from the Church if it creates a false dichotomy between Scripture and the teaching of the Church.

The attitude of the pastor of the parish can be very important in causing or easing alienation on the part of Catholic charismatics. If the pastor conveys hostility toward the charismatic renewal and makes Catholic charismatics feel unwelcome in the parish, it is not surprising that feelings of alienation often follow. This is not to place all the blame on the pastor, or excuse alienation as a justified reaction. It is to say that most Catholics are influenced by the attitude of the pastor, and deeply feel any rejection by him. For many Catholics, the pastor represents the Church. His attitude and actions are hence quite important.

Another cause of alienation is an explicit call to leave one's church and worship with like-minded believers. This call—an old temptation throughout Christian history—is sometimes called "come-out-ism": "come out of your carnal Church into the true fellowship of Spirit-filled believers.'' Its echoes are sometimes heard by charismatic Catholics. Come-out-ism is a false call that the overwhelming majority of charismatic Catholics have rejected. But it can be a persuasive call in some particular situations—when an apparently vibrant charismatic fellowship exists in a town, and the local Catholic Church seems indifferent to what the Spirit is doing today.

Catholics involved in the charismatic renewal are called to be more a part of the Church, not less. This is not a call to stay within the Church primarily to renew it: such an attitude would betray an assumption on our part of superiority over the Church. Rather, the call to Catholics is to remain obedient members of the Church because that is Christ's call. The Church is the way Christ has provided for us to share his life.

This does not mean that we should not pray and work for the renewal of the Church. We should; every Catholic should. However, our primary reason for being a member of the Church should not be merely tactical—a desire to ''work for renewal from within.'' Our call is first of all to be members of the Church, committed to it in mind and heart. Only secondarily are we to be concerned about changing the Church. The charismatic renewal must remain faithful to this primary call, and only secondarily see itself as an instrument of renewal—as important as this renewal might be.

Sometimes the cause of alienation in a parish is a very practical one: having an effective prayer group requires that members spend time they would otherwise give to the parish attending to the prayer groups's needs. The leaders of prayer groups will often lack the time to be very actively involved in their parishes, an understandable situation for leaders. But other members of prayer groups often unconsciously model themselves on their leaders. If the leaders are not actively involved in parish work, other members of the group may likewise drift away. To guard against this danger, leaders should provide regular teaching about the importance of participating in the parish.

Sometimes alienation can be caused by attitudes of elitism. In response to the personal and spiritual benefits we have received from involvement in the charismatic renewal, some charismatics can feel superior to Catholics who are not active in the renewal. It may be true that our Christian lives are more vibrant than before, and it may be true that other Catholics could benefit from similar involvement in the charismatic renewal. But any feeling that we are superior to "un-Spirit-filled" Catholics is sinfully mistaken. Any two-tier view of the Church—"we who are Spirit-filled and those who aren't"—can only weaken identity with the Church. The elite Catholics view fellow Catholics, not as fellow Christians, but as targets for evangelism. The almost inevitable result of such a view is some degree of alienation from other Catholics and from the Church.

If other Catholics perceive that we tend to view them as "unsaved," their reaction is understandably likely to be negative. Often they will reject the charismatic renewal as a misguided movement; sometimes they will personally reject the individuals who have become involved in the charismatic renewal. In turn, this rejection by other Catholics can foster a persecution complex among charismatics. "We were expecting persecution, and sure enough, here it is." A persecuted charismatic tends to interpret events as expressions of rejection. "They didn't elect me to the parish council because I'm involved in the charismatic renewal." Perhaps—or perhaps there were other reasons. But if we allow ourselves to succumb to a persecution complex, then anything less than wholehearted endorsement by others can be used to feed it.

Both a superiority complex and its frequent companion, a persecution complex, can foster feelings of alienation from the parish. Both work directly against the unity that the charismatic renewal is called to seek.

This discussion of the various forms and causes of alienation is not meant to suggest that a massive alienation of charismatic Catholics from the Church is taking place. To the contrary, Catholics involved in the charismatic renewal normally show an increased loyalty to the Church, a renewed appreciation of the sacraments, and a greater involvement in Church life. One sociological study found that there was no evidence that Catholic charismatics were tending to leave the Church, and that there was evidence for just the opposite trend.

However, alienation remains a danger, and both the leaders in the charismatic renewal and the pastors of the Catholic Church must be alert to prevent it. Alienation must be a concern not because it is a prevalent pattern today, but because any degree of alienation works against the basic vision of the charismatic renewal: to become fully integrated into the life of the Church.

Leaders in the charismatic renewal need to be sensitive to the slightest tendencies toward alienation among those they serve, and take steps to correct them. These steps may include working to bridge misunderstandings, counseling individual Catholics on their relation to the Church, providing teaching to the prayer group about the nature of the Church and its place in God's plan, and developing ways in which members of prayer groups can become more involved in parish life. Just as the possible causes of alienation are many, so the steps to be taken to counteract them will be different.

Parish pastors also need to be eager to integrate the charismatic renewal into parish life, and to take steps to prevent alienation of charismatic Catholics from the parish. A pastoral attitude of "If I ignore them, perhaps they will go away" can only increase the chances that they might go away—at least go their separate ways and not become fully involved in parish life.

What is necessary on all sides is a shared vision that the goal is one of integration. Parish pastors and prayer group leaders should agree that any alienation that might occur needs to be resolved. If there is agreement about the goal, and agreement about the undesirability of alienation, then appropriate specific steps can be worked out in each parish to attain the goal and avoid the danger.

Division

Sometimes disunity happens because the parish divides over the charismatic renewal. Charismatically involved Catholics may feel and act fully a part of the parish, but they may nevertheless become the focus of division. Sometimes other parishioners feel threatened by the presence and involvement of Catholic charismatics, and two factions will form in the parish.

Division is not a uniquely charismatic contribution to parish life. In many parishes, Catholics are already divided into factions around many issues: those who desire rapid change in the Church are divided from those who want things left the way they were; those who support strong Catholic schools are divided from those who want more resources put into religious education programs; those who want to take Communion in the hand are divided from those who don't want to. Sometimes these divisions lie beneath the surface of what appears to be a peaceful parish. Sometimes they break out into open disunity. The charismatic renewal is only one of the possible issues around which a parish can divide.

Sometimes the division between charismatically involved parishioners and other parishioners will simply focus on matters unique to the charismatic renewal: prayer meetings, tongues, spiritual gifts, etc. In other cases, the situation may be much more complex, particularly if the charismatic renewal has begun to have an impact on parish life. For example, if charismatics are publicly involved in liturgical renewal in the parish, then the issues causing division might be not only the charismatic renewal, but also changes in the liturgy, laymen distributing Communion, Communion in the hand, etc. While these matters may have little specific relationship to the charismatic renewal, they may be among the causes of division—simply because those who are known to be involved in the charismatic renewal are associated with them.

Similarly, charismatics may become identified as the group that is trying to keep the parish school open (or close the parish school), and could find themselves in a controversy with those who are trying to close the parish school (or keep it open). Again, the issue dividing the parish would not simply be the charismatic renewal, but a disagreement about the role of the parish in education. This is a disagreement charismatics can become involved in simply because they are involved in parish life.

Thus we can see that division in the parish involving Catholic charismatics is sometimes not a simple matter at all, but is greatly complicated by other divisions in the parish. The answer is not for charismatics to shun involvement in the parish but to confront and deal with division in parish life in all its complexity.

However, the charismatic renewal itself can cause division in many ways. Sometimes the problem is simply and basically a lack of accurate information: other Catholics hear rumors about the weekly prayer meeting and do not understand what they hear. It is human to mistrust and be threatened by that which we do not understand. Obviously the charismatic renewal can strike people as being unusual, exotic, even weird if described in incomplete terms.

The answer to this form of division is simple: we must not isolate ourselves from other parishioners, but instead seek opportunities to be with them on an informal basis. The primary aim must not be to evangelize them, but to get to know them on a person-to-person basis. We should not overlook the importance of parish social affairs such as dinners, picnics, dances, and potlucks. Normal social acquaintance should dispel the notion that charismatics are bizarre and unbalanced.

Christianity is not meant to be a strictly otherworldly religion bringing people together only for prayer. The

Body of Christ is built through friendships as well as through prayer meetings, through informal social contact as well as formal liturgies. Friendship often breaks down polarization between parishioners. "It's OK for you to pray differently than I do—because now I know you." Friendship and human understanding is the best basis for an explanation of the charismatic renewal.

Sometimes a parish divides because the charismatic renewal seems to include doctrinal or cultural elements that are "unCatholic." Rarely, in fact, do Catholic charismatics fall into real doctrinal error. But often the forms of prayer and expression used by charismatics appear strange to traditional Catholics, and are in fact culturally foreign to mainstream Catholicism. Catholic charismatics who have learned to be comfortable with loud praise in tongues, clapping with upraised hands, and dancing in the Spirit should remember that these forms still look strange to a Catholic who encounters them for the first time. Even though many Catholics know that Pope Paul VI welcomed the charismatic renewal to Rome, their first visit to a parish prayer group is likely to include some culture shock. This cultural difference can be a point of division, separating those who automatically raise their arms in prayer from those who, as one observer put it, "wouldn't raise their hands over their heads in church if the roof was falling in."

The forms of prayer used by a parish prayer group should be examined to see if they are serious causes of division in its specific situation. If they are, and if another more acceptable but equally valid form of prayer could be adopted instead, it should be. Style of prayer should not be confused with worth of prayer. It is important that prayer be properly expressive. Indeed, the charismatic renewal is called to introduce new forms of prayer into the Church. However, no single style of prayer is irreplaceably essential.

The language some Catholic charismatics use can be equally divisive. Charismatic jargon can be a barrier to unity in the parish. Sometimes the expressions used are merely unfamiliar to most Catholics. Phrases like, "I had a real anointing" and "Let's pray for his deliverance" make the charismatic renewal sound like an exotic, in-group movement. Other forms of expression are dangerously misleading if taken literally—"Has he received the baptism yet?" "Where can I find a Spirit-filled priest?" Such expressions seem to imply distinctions among Christians.

Catholic charismatics have an obligation to speak as intelligibly as possible to other Catholics. Substitutes can be found for all jargon expressions and technical terms. Even the expression, "the baptism of the Holy Spirit" is not irreplaceable: St. Paul never used it in his letters, despite his extensive teaching on finding new life in the Holy Spirit. It is important to determine the impact of language in a particular situation. If our language and forms of expression confuse others, we should try to change the way we speak.

Sometimes overzealous or overaggressive attempts at evangelizing fellow Catholics can cause division in a parish. Most Catholics will not know how to react if they are asked whether they have "been saved." Some Catholics will deeply resent any implication that they haven't been. Probably nothing could divide a parish more quickly than for members of the prayer group to thrust tracts at parishioners as they leave Sunday mass.

Many Catholics do need evangelizing. But they should not be approached as if they were pagans, told that their whole previous lives as Catholics have been pointless, and then promised something sounding like a gimicky salvation. Fellow Christians must be viewed primarily as fellow Christians, not as candidates for evangelism. There is a way of sharing a new-found fullness of life in the Spirit with them that does not show scorn for their lives as devout Catholics. But any simplistic division of the world into two classes of people—the "saved" (us) and the "unsaved" (them)—can only cause division, and make it much more difficult for fellow Catholics to be open to the fuller life that the Holy Spirit is offering them.

The most deadly source of division within a parish is elitism. If we appear to other Catholics as considering ourselves to be the elect of God, the only real Christians in the parish, serious division is almost inevitable. Pushing the charismatic renewal on reluctant friends, parishioners, and pastors will not work. Assuming an elitist air, a messianic complex, an attitude that "we alone have the truth," can undo any good that the Lord wishes to work through the movement. If we view our pastors as "un-Spirit-filled" and insist on our way as *the* way, we will quickly isolate ourselves and discredit the Spirit's work. Fortunately, extreme or blatant forms of elitism are rare in the charismatic renewal. But even tinges of elitism must be recognized as working directly against the plan of God for the charismatic renewal.

Elitism is a natural temptation: most participants in the charismatic renewal are conscious of having received extraordinary love and graces from God. Many can look back on a "pre-charismatic" time when their lives were aimless or disordered, and when they were generally very unhappy. They are very thankful for God's intervention in their lives through the charismatic renewal, and understandably wish everyone could experience the love of God as they do. Thus, attitudes which may strike others as charismatic elitism may be only a deeply felt thankfulness for what God has done and a zealous desire that everyone be transformed by the saving power of the Spirit.

Catholic charismatics must direct their thankfulness and zeal properly and avoid the appearance of elitism. This is a task they share with other renewal movements. In 1975, Bishop Joseph Hogan of Rochester, New York summed up this point in a section of a diocesan pastoral letter addressed to "Renewal Groups," a term Bishop Hogan used to include the Marriage Encounter and Cursillo movements along with the charismatic renewal. He commended these renewal movements: "There is a great spiritual hunger in our times and you, perhaps more than any other groups in the Church, struggle to respond to that hunger. I do not know where we would be without the special gifts you have in this area." He also addressed a word of guidance:

Be careful of a tendency to set yourself and your ways as the norm of what constitutes a fully developed Christian today. You offer a rich and fruitful approach to Christian living but your way is one among many others. Do not use your special graces as a means of judging others and finding them wanting. You have the graces you possess because you are called to service of others. Therefore, I expect all renewal groups to develop proposals for assisting parishes.

There is no simple answer to the problem of division. Rather, there are a number of factors that must go into bringing unity to a parish:

1. Those involved in the charismatic renewal must thirst for unity. We cannot be content with division, or accept it as inevitable.

2. We must make continual efforts to initiate and maintain good communications within the parish. Much disunity springs from misunderstandings. If the pastor is not involved in leadership of the charismatic prayer group, leaders of the prayer group and the pastor should meet for discussions regularly. The parish council should be kept informed of what is happening. We should seek out those in the parish who mistrust or misunderstand us, and try to resolve the difficulties in a non-threatening way. If there is division in the parish over the charismatic renewal, those involved in the renewal should assume the initiative for bringing unity again, and not wait for others to act first.

3. Those involved in the charismatic renewal need to be aware of the impact of what they do on the rest of the parish. They need to be sensitive to others' reactions. This does not mean charismatics must "tone everything down" to make it more acceptable, or abandon use of the spiritual gifts in order to be "less different." However, charismatic Catholics must be sensitive to where the rest

of the parish stands, and be concerned that everything be done to build up the Body of Christ. For example, if a Catholic parish has little experience with ecumenical matters, it would be unwise to invite a flamboyant independent evangelist to conduct a revival meeting in the parish hall. While such a speaker could deliver a stirring message, his presence would most likely be upsetting to many in the parish. The overall effect of his visit might be a negative one, creating division rather than fostering the work of renewal in the parish.

4. Focus on what is primary in the charismatic movement, not what is secondary or accidental. Stress the common Catholicism that all members of the parish share, not the differences between charismatics and other Catholics. Place the emphasis on Jesus Christ, not on the charismatic renewal; on the importance of prayer, not on praying in tongues; on the Church as the Body of Christ, not on the gifts which are meant to build up the Church.

5. Recognize plurality in the Body of Christ. Charismatics need to believe in the full variety of charismatic gifts, not just in those gifts which are most commonly associated with the charismatic renewal. "Charismatics" are not the only charismatics; members of the charismatic renewal are not the only ones to be equipped by God for service. Recognize that our parishes are made up of people who are at different levels of faith and experience, moving at different rates. Each is called to grow into an ever more mature expression of Christ's life; not all are called to leap to the place where we personally are at. Finally, recognize that the charismatic renewal is an authentic working of the Holy Spirit—but

not his only working in the Church today. All are called to live the life of the Spirit; not all are called to the particular form of Christian life represented by the current charismatic renewal. There is one call from Christ to us, one way to the Father through Christ, one Spirit given in baptism—but there are many ways of living out this call, many paths along the way, many manifestations of the Spirit.

Our basic perspective must be one of humility. Humility is not a false sense of unworth; it is a recognition of proper worth. Only as the charismatic renewal recognizes its proper worth with humility will it be able to foster unity in the Church today.

4

Guidance, Prayer, Service

Three elements should be present if the charismatic renewal is to be integrated into the parish and if the parish is to be renewed in the power of the Spirit. These are: the guidance of the Holy Spirit; steadfast prayer and intercession for the parish; and service to the parish.

Guidance, prayer, and service are not magic answers. Nor do they exhaust all of the elements of charismatic parish renewal. They are starting points—keys to open the door to everything that needs to be done to integrate the charismatic renewal into parish life. It would be difficult to imagine the charismatic renewal having a significant effect on the parish without guidance, prayer, and service being fundamental elements.

Guidance

The great diversity of both Catholic parishes and charismatic prayer groups precludes any simple set of instructions for integrating the charismatic renewal into parish life. Each situation is unique. The charismatic renewal will take different forms in different settings. Its relationship to the parish will develop in various ways —all drawing upon general principles and approaches, but each adapted to the individual circumstance. The way we determine how the charismatic renewal should affect a parish is through the guidance of the Lord.

In seeking the Lord's guidance, one of the factors to consider is the nature of the particular parish. Some parishes seem to be thriving under the active leadership of an able pastor. The liturgy is well celebrated; adult education programs are well attended; parish organizations are flourishing; a spirit of enthusiasm pervades parish life. By contrast, other parishes seem to be languishing, with declining attendance at mass, dwindling participation in parish activities, and a general mood of apathy characterizing everything. Some parishes are located in declining "inner-city" settings, with dwindling membership and weakening financial support. Others are located in affluent suburbs, and enjoy a growing membership and a budget surplus.

The approach to the charismatic renewal in a thriving middle-class parish will differ from the approach in an inner-city parish with a small and declining membership. The approach in a lively parish already experiencing various kinds of renewal must be different from the approach in a parish which has yet to feel the effects of Vatican II. The approach in a parish where the pastor solidly supports the charismatic renewal must be different from the approach in a parish where the pastor is openly hostile to it.

Since parishes do not stand alone but are part of dioceses, the stance of the diocese toward the charismatic renewal must also be taken into account. The approach to the charismatic renewal in any parish must respect the diocesan context. Some bishops have openly encouraged the charismatic renewal in their dioceses, sponsored charismatic retreats for their priests, and appointed someone to serve as liaison with prayer groups. Other bishops have been much less supportive of the charismatic renewal. Whatever the bishop's attitude toward the charismatic renewal, it is important for Catholic prayer groups to be in a good relationship with him. They should adhere to any guidelines he may have issued and keep him well informed of all their activities.

Another important factor to consider when seeking the Lord's guidance is the nature and resources of the prayer group. These differ greatly. Some groups are quite large, and are blessed with strong and stable leadership. Other groups are small and struggling, with no acknowledged leaders or anyone willing to assume the responsibility of leadership. Some groups are entirely Catholic in their composition; others are highly ecumenical. Some groups have made mistakes in the past in relating to other Catholics and are viewed as highly suspect in the parish; others are respected and accepted as a part of parish life.

A large cohesive group with able leadership can attempt more ambitious tasks than a newer and weaker group can. What an all-Catholic group meeting in one parish can do might be inappropriate for a city-wide ecumenical group. What might be a realistic load of service within a parish for a large group might exhaust the resources of a smaller group.

A primary question which the prayer group must ask is: to what extent should the group aim at renewing a parish, and to what extent should it focus its efforts on

simply being a good prayer group. It may be premature
for a prayer group to become an agent of change in the
parish; it may need to give priority to its own development until it has ample resources and gifts to offer the
parish. The group may need to ask its only competent
teacher to present a Life in the Spirit Seminar rather than
teach a CCD course for the parish. We should not
forget that simply being a good prayer group and in-
fluencing the lives of individuals is in itself a contribution
to the mission of the Church. While the ultimate goal is
to achieve integration of the charismatic renewal and the
mainstream of Church life, sound and healthy prayer
groups are in themselves valuable for the Church.

Thus, the specific approach to the charismatic renewal
in each parish must be shaped by the uniqueness of that
particular prayer group, parish, and diocese. No set of
principles comprise *the* blueprint to success. No prayer
group can identically duplicate any other group's "success story." General principles and approaches provide
some degree of guidance, and there is much to learn from
the successes (and failures) of others. But in the final
analysis, the path of the Lord for each group and each
parish must be individually discerned.

This point deserves emphasis, because we tend to imitate others, particularly those others whom we view as
successful. If we hear of a nearby prayer group that has
decided to make a covenant commitment, we naturally
wonder if our group should do the same. If someone tells
us how a new pastor and pastoral team successfully
brought the charismatic renewal to a previously dying
parish, we naturally wonder if the same thing could hap-

pen in our parish. It *is* important to learn from the experience and wisdom of others, and to be alert to what God might be asking of us next. But it is also important to respond to what God is asking of *us,* and not merely attempt to imitate what was successful elsewhere.

Therefore, receiving God's guidance is all-important; we need to know his path for *us.* Given the complexity of the parish situations that most prayer groups must confront, and in face of the magnitude of the challenge of renewing parish life in the power of the Spirit, it is doubtful that many of us could successfully discover for ourselves the correct path to follow. Determining how to bring a renewal in the power of the Spirit to our parishes presents an urgent need for the guidance of the Holy Spirit. No matter how helpful general principles and the experience of others may be, we must ultimately discern God's will for us and our parish.

Not only is it important to discern *what* God wants done; it is also important to discern *when* he wants it done. The Lord's timing is crucial.

We find a good example of this principle in Chapter 17 of I Chronicles, the story of David's desire to build a temple for the Lord. To everyone, building a temple clearly seemed to be the right thing to do. The Israelites no longer were a nomadic people, migrating about the Middle East in their tents. They had settled into the promised land, established their cities, and built their houses. It was no longer fitting to keep the ark of the covenant in a tent. And it made sense for David to be the one to build the temple, since the people had been firmly established in their possession of the land through his leadership. Even Nathan, God's chief prophet to Israel at that time, agreed with David's plan to build the temple.

Yet God's word to David was different: "Yahweh says this: You are not the man to build me a house to dwell in" (1 Chron. 17:4). Although David had the best of motives, and although God indeed wanted a temple to be built, God's timing for the temple had not yet arrived.

Premature attempts often fail. And after a project or effort has failed, it is often more difficult to try again and succeed later, when the time is finally right. The Lord told the apostles to preach the gospel to the ends of the earth—but first to wait in Jerusalem for the power of the Holy Spirit to come upon them.

We need to seek God's plan for our parish. We need to seek his will, not only about what to do but when to do it. We need to wait on the Lord, until his timing is right. This does not mean we should be timid or merely cautious. It does mean seriously seeking the guidance of God, and waiting until we receive it.

Fortunately, the charismatic renewal has had much experience in hearing the Lord and receiving guidance from him; this is one area where the charismatic renewal has a contribution to make to the life of the Church. The charismatic renewal is experiencing the truth of God's promise that he intends to provide guidance for his people. We have not been abandoned as orphans and left to muddle through our difficulties as best we can. We do not have to work everything out by ourselves. We can expect to receive help in making important and difficult decisions; we can confidently know that the guidance of the Holy Spirit is available to us. It is sufficient here to merely touch on a few key points about receiving the guidance of the Holy Spirit; other books have dealt with guidance more extensively, notably Stephen Clark's *Knowing God's Will.*

Receiving guidance from God does not mean that we suspend our own reason and understanding and demand miraculous signs to determine our decisions. It does not mean waiting passively for God to make his will known. We have a role to play—a role which calls upon our full capabilities of reason and judgment, which draws upon our experience and the experience of others, which demands we use our common sense.

But our reason, judgment, experience, and common sense are insufficient in themselves to reveal the Lord's direction. We cannot neglect the way the Spirit will speak to us and guide us through his own sovereign action. If many parish councils, parish school boards, pastoral planning teams, and other groups in the Church have had disappointing results, it is in part because they have proceeded exclusively by the power of human wisdom and have not effectively sought God's guidance as a group. No group within the Church—be it a prayer group or a parish council—can afford to act on purely human impulses and techniques when reaching decisions and charting paths.

Some basic points about seeking guidance in knowing how to integrate the charismatic renewal into parish life are:

1. We must seek God's will, not our own. We must put our own desires and inclinations second to his; we must set aside our own preferences and advantage in favor of his will. We cannot receive God's guidance very

well if our minds are preoccupied with ourselves, and our wills are set on having our own way.

2. We must come before the Lord in prayer. If we are seeking God's will, then we must turn to him. The center of gravity of our decision-making must shift from thought to prayer, from our needs to his presence, from wrestling with difficulties to confidently placing the entire matter in his hands. We must seek the Lord in prayer, not as a routine thing to be done before getting down to the real business at hand, but as the most important component in receiving guidance.

3. We should seek guidance as a group, and not merely as individuals. The Lord's will is best discerned by a group of leaders rather than by a single "prophetic" leader. The more we submit our own leadings to others, the more sure we are that we are indeed hearing the Lord clearly and correctly.

4. We should bring all our resources of reason, judgment and experience to bear on the problem. God intends to enlighten our minds, not compensate for our willful stupidity. It is essential to talk things over, to consider alternatives, to weigh the pros and cons of any possible course of action. We should expect God's guidance to emerge in the course of prayerful deliberations.

5. We should be open to prophetic messages and leadings—and take them seriously enough to test them. We should place ourselves in the prayerful attitude which allows God to speak to us through prophecy, and ask him to do so. We should respect the gift of prophecy that has been given to our group, and desire that it mature. However, we should rarely take a single dramatic prophecy as *the* word from the Lord; prophecies that

indicate which course of action to take should receive even more careful scrutiny and testing than is normally necessary.

6. We should be slow to ask for special signs or "set out fleeces." We should also be slow to respond to dramatic and unexpected "miraculous" signs as indicating God's will for us. God has used visions, voices, and marvels to indicate his will—but such are not his normal manner of communicating with man and should not be sought or accepted as such.

7. We should be particularly alert to signs of where the Holy Spirit is already at work. We should follow the path of *his* action, rather than demanding that he bless *our* actions. For example, a prayer group's major effort in youth ministry may have attracted few young people. On the other hand, an offhand announcement about members of the group being willing to visit the sick in their homes and pray with them may have led to a deluge of requests. If the visits have had very good results, this would seem to indicate that the Lord is calling the group more to service of the sick than to service of youth. When seeking guidance, we need to discern what the Lord is doing in our midst, and align our plans with his.

It would be ironic for the charismatic renewal to bring a renewed wisdom about receiving God's guidance to the Church—and yet itself fail to seek God's guidance in bringing charismatic renewal to the parish. The first step for any group that wishes to set about parish renewal must be to come before the Lord with great steadfastness, and seek his will for its specific situation.

We can confidently pray that the grace of God will

enlighten our reason. We can confidently pray that God will give us the discernment to understand situations from a perspective greater than our own. We can confidently pray that God will guide us in the decisions we make if we join together in placing them in his hands.

Prayer

In preparing to write this book, I asked a number of people "what is the most important thing to do to integrate the charismatic renewal into parish life?" One of them replied, "Pray, pray, pray."

Intercessory prayer for the parish is absolutely essential. Prayer is vital because the Church is not merely a human reality, but is the presence of the Lord among his people. For the Church to carry out its mission successfully, it needs not merely human effort, but "a demonstration of the power of the Spirit" (1 Cor. 2:4). Thus, when we are engaged in the work of parish renewal, we are not merely trying to make a human reality less imperfect. We are entering into God's plan for the salvation of the world.

Our access to the power of God is through Jesus Christ in prayer. In the charismatic renewal we have experienced the truth of Jesus' teaching, "Ask, and you shall receive" (Luke 11:9). We have experienced in our time what the apostles experienced when they prayed for the power of the Holy Spirit: as their prayers were answered, "the house where they were assembled rocked" (Acts 4:31). We have seen that prayer does make a difference.

Our parishes must become one of our foremost prayer concerns. We need to pray for our pastor and our other parish leaders. Our prayer for them should not be a "loaded" prayer: "Oh Lord, wake Father Smith up to the truth and get him to join our prayer group. We know you can do it, Lord; we know you can save him." Rather, our prayer must respect God's love for our pastor and honor his place in God's plan. Our prayer must be a prayer of humility: not that our pastor "catch up with us," but that God will continue to equip him for service as pastor and will love him as a son.

We should also pray for specific needs of the parish. Sometimes these needs are obvious; sometimes it may take some discernment to uncover them. Usually the pastor is the person who knows the needs of the parish most acutely. If he has any degree of openness at all to the charismatic renewal, we may simply approach him with the question: "Father, we want to pray regularly for the parish and its needs. What would you like us to pray for?"

We should also pray that the charismatic renewal would play its proper role in the parish. Partly this will be a prayer for guidance, but it will also be a prayer that the Lord's plan for renewal of the parish in the power of the Spirit will unfold. If divisiveness over the charismatic renewal is an actual or potential problem, we might pray specifically for unity. If the parish is generally closed to the charismatic renewal or afraid of it, we might pray to find ways to serve the parish and its people. We might ask the Lord to pour abundant gifts of pastoral ministry to the parish. We might pray for the parish council. We may pray that an atmosphere of peace will pervade the parish.

We should particularly ask the Lord to work with power in our parish, touching lives, changing lives, drawing all to himself. The Body of Christ is not a human invention: the Holy Spirit brings it into being in our midst. A parish is renewed not merely by good will and hard work, but by the Holy Spirit bringing men and women alive in Christ. We need to pray that the Holy Spirit will touch the life of every parishioner, equipping each for his or her unique call as a Christian, and uniting us all in love. At its root, the charismatic renewal is a reminder that each of us needs to be touched by the power of the Spirit. Our prayer should be a prayer that this happens.

In some situations, intercessory prayer for the parish may be all that a prayer group can do and should do in the parish. If the pastor adamantly opposes the charismatic renewal, the group should probably make no overt efforts to renew the parish. It may even be unwise to try to change the pastor's mind. The only course of action open may be to intercede for the parish, and beseech the Lord to bring it peace and unity.

We should not denigrate the value of intercessory prayer, even if this is sometimes all a group can do to bring renewal to the parish. Prayer is essential. It is the basis for any renewal. We tend to place too much importance on the value of our own efforts, and not to rely enough on the power of God to change situations. We are too easily tempted to feel thwarted and to give up if our efforts at renewal do not gain ready acceptance. Instead we should rely firmly on the power of prayer.

One of the first parishes in the United States to experience a renewal in the power of the Spirit was the Episcopal Church of the Redeemer in Houston, Texas. In many ways, the Church of the Redeemer is a unique situation. It was a dying parish in a racially changing neighborhood; as a weak parish, it was thus open to a radically new direction and dynamic leadership. Further, it received this remarkable leadership from Rev. Graham Pulkingham and the men who gathered around him. But the initial impetus to the parish's renewal was prayer —the steadfast prayer of one person. Long before renewal came to the Church of the Redeemer, Grace Murray, a parishioner, became involved in the charismatic renewal. She was openly ridiculed by other parishioners, and was tempted to leave the parish. But she believed that the Holy Spirit wanted her to "stay and pray," and stay and pray she did. After some years of her persistent prayer, Graham Pulkingham was sent to the Church of the Redeemer as its new pastor, and 15 months later his ministry was transformed by the power of the Holy Spirit. Then began the dramatic change: a dying inner-city parish became a dynamic Christian community. This story of the Church of the Redeemer has been told by Graham Pulkingham in his books, *Gathered for Power* and *They Left Their Nets,* and by Michael Harper in *A New Way of Living*. But it is important to remember that in a significant sense this story began with the steadfast prayer of one woman.

Catholic charismatics can intercede for their parish both as individuals and as a group. If we are serious about bringing renewal to our parish, it should be our daily prayer concern. If we are committed as a group to becoming a part of the parish, it should be reflected in the way we pray together. Our prayer should be humble, not triumphal. It should be a prayer modeled on Mary's: "I am the handmaid of the Lord. Let his will be carried out in me."

Service

The third key to the integration of the charismatic renewal into the parish is involvement in roles of service.

Serving the parish is more than a matter of strategy or tactics. At its root, our desire to serve is an expression of our desire to imitate Christ. "I am in your midst as he who serves" (Luke 22:27). A desire to serve must form the bond of the life of any community. If we wish that our parishes were stronger communities, then we should take the first step ourselves by laying down our own lives in service. We are not called to stand aloof, idly wish for renewal, and criticize the state of the parish.

Catholic parishes will have varying degrees of openness to the charismatic renewal. Under the leadership of the pastor, some parishes may wholeheartedly welcome the charismatic prayer group and embrace the involvement of charismatics in the parish. Other parishes are less open and are generally uncertain about how to respond to the charismatic renewal. However, even pastors and parishioners who are dubious about the charismatic renewal as a movement may be open to the involvement of charismatics in roles of service in the parish.

Where parishes are suspicious of the charismatic renewal, adopting roles of unassuming service is the least threatening and most helpful action that a prayer group can take. If a parish is seriously divided over the charismatic renewal, humble service offers the greatest hope for achieving unity. If a pastor opposes the charismatic renewal, patiently serving the parish in ways he can appreciate may be the only feasible course of action.

True service must be based on the needs of those to be served. We do not serve others to meet *our* needs; we serve them to meet *their* needs. We must serve on others' terms, not on our own.

Nevertheless, we should realize that some parish activities have less intrinsic value than others. We should be most eager to serve in ways which directly aid the mission of the Church. For example, it is ordinarily preferable to expend ourselves visiting the sick and elderly rather than by selling raffle tickets door-to-door. At the same time, we need a spirit of service that will free us to pitch in where we are needed—even if it means setting up chairs in the parish hall or carrying out trash.

Jesus gave us the supreme example of humble service when he washed the apostles' feet. This job was normally done by a household slave; it was not a specifically "religious" act. Yet Jesus did not consider it beneath his dignity to wash his apostles' feet, nor did he scorn the act as not being "religious." To the contrary, he showed us that humble, self-sacrificing service lay at the heart of the good news and the coming of the kingdom. He explicitly told the apostles to do as he did: "I have given you an example so that you may copy what I have done to you" (John 13:15). Likewise, when serving in our parishes, we should be slow to reject jobs as being beneath our dignity or not "religious" enough to merit our attention.

In serving, we must be sensitive to the general mood of the parish. Some parishioners may be fearful of "the pentecostals taking over the parish." Quiet roles of service may well be preferable to public positions of power. It may be wiser to volunteer for jobs which no one else wants, rather than to run for the parish council, simply to avoid all appearance of wanting to "take over." Neither, however, should we shun serving on the parish council if that role of service is available.

As we move toward new areas of service in the parish, it is important to balance our new commitments with responsibilities we already have. Confronted by the chronic unmet needs of most parishes, it would be all too easy to so immerse ourselves in parish activities to the detriment of our other obligations to family, prayer, and job. We must prayerfully seek the right balance between service within our homes and service outside our homes, between parish involvement and prayer group involvement.

We must also take care to determine the right area of parish service for *us*. We should know from our involvement in the charismatic renewal that the Body of Christ includes a variety of roles of service and that different individuals receive different gifts to carry them out. Not everyone has the gift to teach at prayer meetings. Similarly, not everyone is equipped to teach religious education on the junior high level, and not everyone is equipped to be a lector. But experience in the charismatic renewal also teaches us that everyone is equipped for some role of service. No member of the body is without his function, his distinctive contribution to the good of the whole. Our task is to seek out those areas of service that we have been equipped to perform.

In the typical parish, many needs for service are chronically unmet, and many of these services are ideal for those involved in the charismatic renewal to perform. The following listing only touches on a few of them.

Works of mercy. Jesus has called the Church to have a special concern for the sick, the poor, the handicapped, the elderly, the shut-in, and those unable to provide a dignified life for themselves. Quite often these people most need someone to care: someone who will visit them, drive them to mass on Sunday, do grocery shopping once a week, care for small needs, and thus bear witness to the love of God. Every parish has many members who suffer in quiet need.

Most often what is needed is not money or elaborate organization, but simply people who will extend themselves a little bit in love and service. A telephone call to the pastor, simply asking to be put in touch with people in need is usually all that is necessary to get started.

Religious education. The typical CCD program is usually hard-pressed for enough teachers and teachers' aides for the classes it offers to students at various levels. Teaching CCD is often a very demanding role of service, but one which offers the satisfaction of proclaiming the message of the gospel and helping to form young people in their relationship with Jesus Christ.

However, religious educators and charismatic Catholics sometimes have a tense relationship. On one hand, some religious education programs seem to have replaced the Lordship of Jesus Christ with audio-visual technology. Charismatics and others rightly object to a CCD class which lacks a clear presentation of the gospel. On the other hand, in our eagerness to preach the gospel, we sometimes neglect the valid insights educators have into the psychological development of children. Both groups usually have something to learn from the other. Charismatics can often bring a clear focus on the essentials of Christianity to a religious education program. Religious educators can help us appreciate the stages of development that children go through on their way to adult faith.

Intercessory prayer. Many traditional forms of intercessory prayer have virtually died out in the Church: novenas for peace or health, vigils before the Blessed Sacrament, group rosaries. It would probably be a mistake to try to revive many of these old forms, but in most parishes something should take their place. Intercessory prayer for the needs and mission of the parish is still essential. Ideally this prayer should be done in the church, perhaps as a vigil of intercession open to all parishioners. The forms of prayer used should be comfortable to all parishioners who participate.

Liturgy. The liturgy is an obvious area of service. The pastor—along with the parish's liturgical committee—has the responsibility of shaping the character of the parish liturgy. Within that context, however, there are many roles of service charismatics can perform.

For example, music is often led and sung halfheartedly at mass. Charismatic prayer groups—which typically rely heavily on song as a form of praise and have developed some musical skills—could volunteer to lead the singing at one of the Sunday masses. Even simply joining the choir to strengthen it would be a welcome step in many parishes.

Evangelism. Despite Vatican II's words about the need to spread the gospel, far too little evangelism goes on in the Catholic Church today. The declining numbers of adult converts are one rather dismal indicator of this. Yet about one half of the United States population does not have any church affiliation. The need for evangelism cannot be denied.

Parishes that have any kind of active evangelism program, or are willing to begin one, would likely welcome the participation of those involved in the charismatic renewal.

Ecumenism. Despite the successes of dialogues between Catholic and Protestant theologians, all too little ecumenical contact takes place on the grass roots level. Most Catholic charismatic groups include some Protestants, and some prayer groups are highly ecumenical in their composition. While differences of belief and discipline still divide Christianity, the charismatic renewal provides a common ground for Christians to get together to pray and grow in love for each other.

If the Body of Christ is to one day be reunited, a base of understanding and trust is as necessary as theological agreement. It may take a fair amount of openness and creativity for a parish to draw upon the ecumenical resources that a prayer group may provide, but the potential is often there. Making known to the pastor a willingness to serve in the area of ecumenism would be a good first step.

All these various works and roles of service have one thing in common: by undertaking them, those involved in the charismatic renewal become more personally involved in the parish. The ultimate integration of the charismatic renewal into the parish will come about in part by a thorough integration of charismatic Catholics into parish life. The lofty goal of integration must take flesh and blood form in the way charismatics spend their time and effort.

These forms of service will also contribute to the renewal of parish life. Only a limited amount of renewal can be accomplished by changing exterior forms and procedures. At its heart, parish renewal means individuals living the life of Christ in a fuller way, and performing in a renewed way the very ordinary elements that make up parish life. At its heart, parish renewal means that parishioners are more fully and actively a part of the parish. Those involved in the charismatic renewal should take the lead in doing this—by quietly and humbly going about the tasks and services which form the backbone of parish life.

Service to the parish will not by itself bring about a complete renewal of the parish in the power of the Holy Spirit. Service to the parish cannot do away with the necessity for the pastor's leadership; it cannot replace the sovereign work of the Holy Spirit in touching men's hearts and bringing them to fuller life in Christ; it will not automatically transform parishioners' relationships with each other. Service is necessary for parish renewal, but other elements are necessary as well.

Nevertheless, we should not overlook the importance of service to the parish. If a prayer group functions as a service arm within a parish, it can make a difference in many ways. It can greatly affect the lives of those individuals that it serves: older people, those receiving religious instruction, those who are simply befriended by members of the group. A serving prayer group can also have an impact on the general tone of the parish, particularly in how it worships. Service can establish a good relationship between the prayer group and the parish, as a first step toward the full renewal that the Lord wishes to accomplish.

A prayer group should dedicate itself to service, not for tactical reasons, but because the Lord asks it to serve. Service must be done in obedience to the Lord; lives must be laid down in imitation of he who gave up his life for us. There can be no more basic, or sufficient, reason to serve in our parishes than our desire to imitate Jesus Christ.

The first step in undertaking any role of service should be to approach the pastor and make known our willingness to serve. Ask him what he sees as the chief needs of the parish. Discuss how members of the prayer group could make the greatest contribution to the life and mission of the parish.

Some pastors are fearful of the charismatic renewal, and may be reluctant to draw upon the services of Catholic charismatics. They may be unsure where such service will lead; they may be skeptical about our steadfastness and stability in carrying out a service role; they may simply want to avoid the appearance of endorsing the prayer group. The key to soothing such fears lies in others' perception in us of a genuine desire to serve. We should be available to undertake the roles of service that no one else wants with no strings attached. If we do not have this attitude of heart—if our motives are political, if our desire to serve is only a passing fancy—this too will be detected.

It may not appear to us that our faithfully carrying out a role of parish service is making much difference. "I've been a lector for three months now, and the pastor still won't come to a prayer meeting." We need to believe that our steadfast service does make a difference where it counts—in God's plan for our lives and for the Church. Our call is to be faithful to the many different services the Lord has given us—in our family, in our parish, in our work, in our prayer group. Our faithfulness is the raw material that the Spirit can use to build up the Body of Christ. Our service to our parish can be a key link in integrating the charismatic renewal into the parish, and bringing renewal in the Spirit to the Church.

5

The Role of the Pastor

A dominant conclusion from the informal survey taken in preparation for writing this book was that the pastor is crucial for renewing the parish in the power of the Spirit. Parish renewal cannot be accomplished unless the pastor is functioning in his proper role.

This does not mean that parish renewal depends completely on the work of one man, or that prayer groups should disband if they do not have the enthusiastic endorsement of the pastor. The point that emerged from the survey is that there is a limit to what a prayer group can do to renew the parish if it lacks the support and leadership of the pastor.

The pastor's influence on what happens in the parish should not surprise us. The Second Vatican Council did not attempt to replace the pastor by the parish council, nor has increased involvement by the laity in the Church made the priesthood obsolete. To the contrary, it is a fact of experience that the pastor is the single most important person for determining what will succeed and what will fail in the parish.

Thus, groups which have the support of the pastor will be in a better position to serve the parish than those which

do not have his support. Groups which receive his en-
lightened leadership will be in the best position to undertake the work of renewing the parish. Groups which do
not yet have the pastor's support or leadership must act
within these limitations. They may well have to proceed
very slowly, praying for the parish, and serving it faithfully. The Lord brings renewal in his own time, through
the power of his Spirit.

This chapter will focus on the role of the pastor who
favors the integration of the charismatic renewal into
parish life, and wants to see a renewal of the parish in the
power of the Spirit. The advice offered must be considered tentative: we are only beginning to experience
charismatic parish renewal and we thus have only a preliminary understanding of how pastor and prayer group
should relate to each other.

While this chapter will stress the role of the pastor, it
does not mean that the associate or assistant pastors in a
parish are unimportant or have no role. They too share in
exercising the pastoral function in the parish. They are
(or should be) the first rank of those coresponsible with
the pastor for serving the parish.

The primary function of the pastor of a parish is to be
concerned for the overall good of the parish and of each
member. He must provide direction and leadership, involving others in carrying out the mission of the parish.
He must nurture the growth of the parish into a worshipping community. He must see to it that appropriate pastoral care is available for every member of the parish.

The pastor's function extends far beyond the jobs of
administering the parish and celebrating the sacraments.

In the root meaning of the word "pastor," he is the "shepherd" of the parish: one who provides overall leadership and direction, one who provides for individual care and concern.

One specific implication of this understanding of the pastor's role is that the pastor must be concerned about the *whole* parish. He must be the pastor of both those who are involved in the charismatic renewal and those who are not. He cannot let his private opinion of any group in the parish affect the way he acts as shepherd of those in his charge.

Thus, a pastor wishing to lead his parish toward a renewal in the power of the Spirit must do so while keeping the situation of the whole parish and all the parishioners in mind. He cannot allow the parish to undertake a program of renewal in a way that will alienate a sizeable portion of the parishioners. It will do little good for the pastor to singlemindedly embrace the charismatic renewal if the result will be such serious division and contention in the parish that he can no longer carry out his pastoral ministry to the whole parish. The pastor must be the pastor of all the people.

The pastor's responsibility to be pastor of the whole parish does not mean that he cannot be active in the charismatic renewal and lead the parish into renewal in the power of the Spirit. Similarly, the possibility of division and contention does not mean that the "charismatic" dimension of the charismatic renewal should be suppressed in order to preserve the peace. The point is that the pastor must act tactfully and wisely with regard to the charismatic renewal. He must be sensitive to the mood of the parish and work to educate the parish about the nature of the charismatic renewal.

It should be realized that renewal will not come to a parish simply through the efforts of a prayer group. Many aspects of parish life depend very directly upon the spiritual leadership of the pastor.

The word of God proclaimed and explained from the pulpit during the liturgy is the chief preaching and teaching occasion for the parish. The priest's meditative preparation for his preaching, and his proclamation of the gospel with power, is all-important for making the word of God present to the parish.

The pastor is the point of unity for a parish. Whether a parish is growing in unity depends upon whether the pastor is striving for unity, instructing the parishioners in how broken relationships may be mended, and seeking to personally reconcile different factions. The pastor is not only a mediator between his people and God; he is a mediator among his people. He must prevent factions from forming in the parish, and seek to restore unity if they do form.

One important aspect of the pastor's leadership will be his leadership of the parish council. The council should be a group of men and women gathered around the pastor, concerned with the overall mission of the parish. It should not be a group concerned merely with the business and administrative aspects of parish life. It should be growing in a spiritual vision for the parish. The responsibility for this growth in vision must rest with the pastor—a role he performs by teaching and example rather than by exercise of veto power. When the charismatic renewal begins to have impact on a parish, the council should understand what is happening and be able to support it. This can best happen if the pastor is carrying out his proper role with the council.

The pastor also has unique roles of service to a parish prayer group. His very availability to members of the group and presence in their midst is important. Even if he exercises no other role during a prayer meeting, his very presence there makes a difference.

Many Catholics acknowledge this unique role when they seek the pastor's encouragement and endorsement before they will consider becoming personally involved in the charismatic renewal. They are not looking for an unqualified approval, or a mandate to become involved, but rather the pastor's assessment of this new movement, and his assurance that it is developing in good order with his knowledge. Many Catholics look to their pastors for direction of this kind, and are reluctant to become involved in anything religious that meets with his disapproval.

The pastor also serves the prayer group through his theological training and his function as minister of the sacraments. The pastor's theological background enables him to bring a unique and vital perspective to many questions that will arise as the prayer group develops. Without being a forbidding "watchdog of orthodoxy," the pastor should be able to exercise a guiding role, seeing to it that the prayer group provides sound teaching and avoids common problems.

Whatever the pastor's degree of involvement in the group, Catholic charismatics will turn to him for the sacraments. Whether this is done on an individual basis, or whether he celebrates the liturgy for the prayer group, he is the indispensible source of sacramental life for members of the prayer group.

Sometimes, a pastor can function as a type of "spiritual director" for the parish prayer group, similar to the way he may function as a spiritual director for individuals. A spiritual director helps chart a course toward proper growth in the Christian life. He rarely makes decisions for those he directs; but rather helps others to clarify their spiritual condition and to discern God's will for them. A director guides others through difficulties, not by imposing solutions, but by discerning with them a proper course of action.

A pastor can function this way in relation to a prayer group. He can advise and counsel the leaders, discern with them the group's strengths and weaknesses, and help them determine the proper course of development. He will probably do this by meeting with the leaders of the group. However, he will need to have enough experience with the group as a whole to have a sense of its unique nature and its particular needs.

Needless to say, all of these various functions will take the pastor's time. Indeed, the factor which most often determines how involved a pastor can become with a prayer group is his available time. A pastor may well face a quandry: to bring a renewal to his parish through his involvement in the charismatic renewal may require him to sacrifice some of his other activities. This can be a difficult challenge to already overworked pastors trying to meet many legitimate needs. But there is no way around it: involvement in any depth in the charismatic renewal demands a commitment of time, and it usually requires a reordering of priorities about the use of one's time.

A primary question about the role of the pastor is, "should the pastor of the parish be the leader of the prayer group?" Differences among parish situations (and differences among pastors) make it difficult to answer this question in a simple manner. It also raises other questions about the role of lay leadership in the group, the best way to achieve integration of the prayer group into the parish, and the goal of charismatic parish renewal.

First, two pitfalls need to be avoided. On the one hand, a pastor should not simply "take charge" of a group and make all decisions himself. A pastor's one-man rule can be as much a mistake as a layman's one-man rule. In charismatic groups, team leadership and shared ministry are advisable. One-man rule is almost always a bad idea—even if the one man is the pastor of the parish.

On the other hand, it can be an equally bad mistake for the pastor to have nothing to do with prayer group leadership. The pastor must take an active pastoral role if the prayer group is truly a parish prayer group and wants to become integrated into the parish. Most often the pastor should exercise his pastoral leadership as a key member of the pastoral team responsible for the prayer group, although he might also fulfill this role as an advisor to the team who stays in close touch with what is going on.

The fact that a priest exercises an overall pastoral role for a prayer group does not automatically mean that he should lead prayer meetings. Other members of the pastoral team—lay persons—may be better gifted as prayer meeting leaders. Nor does the pastor's leadership role mean that he automatically does all or most of the teaching at prayer meetings. Pastoral leadership involves a teaching role—but often non-clerical members of the team are particularly gifted in teaching. A priest usually has superior theological training, but this does not mean that the priest is always the most gifted in conveying practical teachings in a clear manner. Theologically trained leaders should participate in *preparing* the teaching, but the most theologically competent person does not have to actually *do* the teaching.

The various functions of leadership and service should be performed by those who have received the proper gifts. We should not expect priests to possess every gift or exercise every role of service necessary to the group. Neither should we automatically look to lay people for all these gifts. The Holy Spirit gives his charisms to priests and laity alike. Some priests may have a gift for inspired preaching; others have gifts of healing, teaching, prophecy, and discernment. All these gifts should be put at the disposal of the parish and the prayer group, along with the gifts of lay people.

Having an overall pastoral role, then, does not mean carrying out all the individual roles of service and leadership. Priests involved in the charismatic renewal need to have enough self-confidence and a good enough self-image that they are not threatened by having other leaders, more gifted in specific areas, play prominent roles. In fact, the pastor can often best carry out his overall pastoral role by functioning as a "coordinator of ministries": one who sees to it that all the various gifts are developed so that all the needs of the group are met. The aim of the overall pastor must be to see to it that worship is led well, not necessarily to lead worship himself; that sound teaching is given, not necessarily to teach himself; that the group is open to the word of the Lord addressed to them in prophecy, not necessarily to be a prophet himself.

This role as coordinator of ministries requires two qualities: an overall concern and vision for the group, and the skill to help develop various gifts and roles of service to meet these needs. The pastor's overall vision will of necessity include a concern that each individual in the group has available the kind of help he needs in order to grow to maturity in the Christian life. Since one man cannot hope to personally meet all these individual needs, he must be concerned that others within the group learn how to provide pastoral care for the members of the group. Thus, having an overall concern for the group must include a concern that members of the group grow to maturity in the use of spiritual gifts and the performance of various roles of service. The needs of the group cannot be met otherwise.

In essence, the pastor's role in the prayer group is the same as his role in the parish. The differences are ones of degree. In both places, the pastor must be concerned that various gifts are developed to meet the needs of the group. He must have an overall vision of God's plan for the group or parish, and he should see to it that leaders and ministries are provided to carry out God's plan.

In viewing the pastor's role, we should keep in mind the importance of coordinated pastoral care. Prayer group leaders will find themselves exercising increasing pastoral responsibilities if the prayer group develops as it should. No longer will the leaders of the prayer group be concerned merely with a weekly prayer meeting. They will be called to serve those in the group in pastoral ways. Such pastoral care should be coordinated with the parish pastor because it would be ultimately unwise for the pastor and the prayer group leaders to become two separate centers of pastoral responsibility within the parish. It is advisable for there to be unity between the pastor and the leaders of the prayer community in offering pastoral care for members of the parish, however co-responsibility and delegation of responsibility are worked out. There can be only one overall pastor in a parish.

What happens, then, when a pastor will have nothing to do with a prayer group, even though the group is healthy and ready to provide pastoral care to its members? Should pastoral care be denied simply because it could only be offered independently of the pastor? This can be a very difficult and painful dilemma. The short-term inclination may be to go ahead and offer whatever help can be provided, despite the uninvolvement of the pastor. However, in the long term, this approach may set up a separate center of pastoral care in the parish and ultimately work against the integration of the charismatic renewal into the parish. The matter is a difficult one, and the guidance of the Spirit must be earnestly sought.

The aim must be unity. The ultimate goal must be integration. The path to this goal may be filled with uneasy compromises. Even if the pastor will not support the prayer group, it is better to keep him informed of what is happening than to sever all communication. And even pastors who are sympathetic and supportive may not have the time to become actively involved with the prayer group and its leadership.

A pastor who is well disposed to the charismatic renewal and wishes to encourage the movement in his parish may encounter one of a number of different situations. The most common are these: 1) no prayer group currently meets within the parish bounds and few parishioners are involved in the charismatic renewal; 2) a prayer group meets somewhere within the parish, but does not have strong ties to the parish; 3) the pastor may be in some role of leadership for a charismatic group within the parish, and is seeking ways in which the group could help bring renewal to the parish. Something brief may be said about each of these situations.

If the pastor wishes to begin a prayer group in a parish which does not have one, he should proceed deliberately. Unless he and other parishioners have had quite extensive previous involvement in the charismatic renewal, it would probably be unwise to simply start a prayer meeting and announce it in the parish bulletin. At first, the pastor should probably encourage parishioners to become active in a nearby prayer group in order to gain experience, and he should become involved along with them. In most parts of the country, an already existing and well-functioning prayer meeting can be found within driving distance of any parish. The pastor could encourage individual parishioners to become involved in the charismatic renewal, explaining it to them and answering their questions. If he hopes the charismatic renewal will become an effective means of renewal in the parish, he should particularly encourage parishioners who might be potential leaders to become involved.

Once a number of parishioners have gained experience attending a nearby prayer meeting on a regular basis for a period of time, it may be possible to begin a *private* prayer meeting within the parish itself. It would probably be a mistake to initially open this meeting to all parishioners. Those already involved should meet among themselves at first, until the group has achieved a level of maturity sufficient to enable it to serve others and introduce them to the charismatic renewal. This core group should have developed gifts of leadership, prophecy, and worship before attempting rapid expansion. This group should also be capable of providing the basic teaching necessary to foster renewal in the Spirit: it should be able to offer the Life in the Spirit Seminars, and it should also provide some kind of ongoing basic post-seminar instruction. All this will require that a leaders team has been formed and has learned how to function well together. The members must know how to submit to one another, how to discern God's will for the group, how to lay down their lives in service to the group. These preliminary steps are essential. A flood of interested parishioners coming to a prayer meeting before an effective core group is functioning can swamp the group, overtax its leaders, and result in a wasted opportunity. Of course leaders should rely on the Lord's strength rather than their own. However, the Lord wishes to build on strong foundations and he asks hard work of us to lay them. Once the foundation has been established, then growth may take place.

If a prayer meeting already exists in a parish but without strong ties to parish life, the first step for a pastor to take is to establish contact with it and its leaders. Even if a pastor does not feel any *personal* attraction to the charismatic renewal, he should acknowledge a responsibility for the group. The concern of the pastor must extend to all individuals and groups within the parish. A charismatic prayer group is not beyond the pastor's care; to the contrary, it needs his care.

If a pastor in this situation knows little about the charismatic renewal he should find out more about the movement. He could talk to other priests who are active in the movement and who know more about it; there are almost certain to be such priests in his own diocese. He could also read some of many books that have been written about the movement; he should invite the leaders of the prayer group to meet with him and describe what is going on in the parish. If the pastor is newly assigned to the parish and finds an already existing group, he should ask the previous pastor for some background and advice. He should also seek the guidance of his bishop if he is in doubt of what course of action to take.

A pastor who is personally involved in the charismatic renewal or who has some role of leadership in a parish prayer group should be concerned about integrating the charismatic renewal into parish life. The pastor should be the key link between the prayer group and the parish.

The pastor in this situation has unique opportunities to encourage people to become involved in the charismatic renewal. He may advise some of the people he is counseling about various difficulties to seek additional help and support in the prayer group, if the prayer group has the resources to serve such people. He might identify leaders in the parish who would have much to offer the prayer group, and encourage them to make contact with it. On the other hand, he might urge members of the prayer group to become involved in the specific works of the parish which he is concerned about. He could take the initiative in bringing members of the prayer group together with individuals who need works of mercy assistance and make many other suggestions that would help the group make a difference in parish life.

The pastor can give quiet endorsement to a prayer group in many undramatic ways. He could make sure that the parish council is kept informed of the activities of the prayer group; put occasional announcements of the time and place of the prayer meeting in the parish bulletin; and choose leaders of the prayer group for liturgical roles such as lector, commentator, and extraordinary minister of the Eucharist. The supportive pastor can appoint prayer group leaders to positions on the spiritual development and Christian service commissions of the parish council, if council by-laws allow him to make appointments. None of these steps are as dramatic as a sermon endorsing the charismatic renewal—but, taken together, they can be effective.

The presence of the pastor at prayer meetings might be more important than any specific role he plays during the meeting. It is not necessary for a pastor to be a "charismatic" figure, prominent in the leadership of the group. His simple presence at the meeting as pastor among his people will make a difference.

At the same time, the pastor should work closely with the leaders of the prayer group. Leaders need ongoing spiritual formation even more than the people that they serve. Many groups will need to rely on the pastor's theological training to steer them clear of an overly literalist approach to Scripture and other hazards. Groups need to rely on the pastor's overall view of the parish and its parishioners in charting the course that they are to take in the parish. The pastor can provide this guidance in many ways. Depending on the circumstances, he might be a member of the pastoral team that serves the prayer group. He might lead it as "pastor of the pastoral team"; he should at least be an advisor staying in close contact with the leaders.

The particular style of involvement and role of leadership the pastor chooses does not in any way change his ultimate role as pastor of the parish. He must be the ultimate source of unity and pastoral vision within the parish. He must be the one who reconciles the diverse groups within the parish, maintaining a healthy plurality while preventing divison. While the pastor shares his responsibilities and ministry with other pastoral leaders in the parish, he must be the ultimate authority in the parish when authority is necessary. If the prayer group is to be rooted in the parish, it must be in ultimate submission to the pastor, as must all parish groups. There should not be two independent lines of pastoral authority within the parish. This does not mean, of course, that the pastor should carry out his role in an authoritarian or arbitrary manner or even that he must make all the important decisions. Rather the point is that the goal of parish renewal in the power of the Spirit requires submission to the pastoral authority set over the parish.

Father Harold F. Cohen, S.J., has drawn up some guidelines on "Priests and the Charismatic Renewal" for use in the New Orleans Archdiocese. They are presented below, in a slightly edited form, as a conclusion and summary of this chapter:

1. The Lord calls all his people to a deep life in the Spirit (John 7:37-39). Priests should be open to this deep life, pray for it (Luke 11:9-13), and follow the lead of the Spirit.
2. Priestly ministry is as necessary to the charismatic renewal as it is to the church at large:
   a) People active in the charismatic renewal need the ministry of priests, especially in the celebration of the sacraments of the Eucharist and of Reconciliation.
   b) Priests as a rule have had more training in theology than most laymen. (Some priests need updating and while some modern theological approaches seem to lessen the role of God's action in history, priests in general are nonetheless better equipped theologically than most laymen.)
   c) In addition to his roles as minister of the sacraments and theological consultant, the priest's discerned gifts should determine what other functions he should exercise in a prayer group as in the local church. Priests, like all members of the body, have their gifts: teaching, preaching, counseling, healing, administration, music, discernment.
3. In charismatic prayer groups, many gifts and ministries are exercised. Common ones are: prophecy,

healing, music, discerning, teaching, pastoring, praying in tongues, and a variety of services.

The pastoring ministry is frequently exercised by a group or team. Its function is to discern where the Lord is calling the group; to discern the gifts and ministries he is giving; to call forth the proper exercise of these gifts and ministries and to coordinate them for the overall good of the group and service to the local church.

To discern and coordinate does not mean to possess all the gifts. It does mean to be open to all the Lord is doing and saying in and through the members of the group and to call the group to the appropriate response.

In the leadership group, no one person will necessarily have all the pastoral gifts. All should have a certain spiritual maturity relative to that of the members of the prayer group. All should have a concern for the spiritual growth of all the members of the prayer group and of the prayer group as a whole. A gift of discernment should be present in all of the leaders. They should also be free from serious psychological or emotional problems.

Other gifts should be present in one or more members of the leadership team: administration, the ability to correct and admonish in a kindly manner, and other gifts. Often there will be teaching and prophetic gifts among them.

An important test that the leaders are truly responding to the lead of the Holy Spirit is their attitude of obedience to the local bishop whose charism it is to discern charisms.

4. From this description of leadership in a charismatic prayer group it should be clear that a priest, by the simple fact that he is a priest, is not thereby qualified to assume a leadership position (other than the leadership implied in administering the sacraments and offering theological counsel to the existing leaders). Such qualifications should be proven, not presumed.

5. Priests, therefore, should *not:*

   a) assume a leadership role in an already existing prayer group unless invited to do so by the leaders;

   b) too readily accept such an invitation until they have had a certain amount of experience in the charismatic renewal. Attending a Life in the Spirit Seminar would be a good first step because this seven-week seminar is a very commonly used and effective means of initating people into the charismatic renewal. The priest should also attend prayer meetings over a period of time, especially meetings of experienced and solid groups; attend leadership and general conferences; talk with experienced leaders; and read the relevant literature about the renewal.

   But the most important steps of all are a deepening union with the Lord Jesus, flowing from an ongoing repentance and deepening commitment; and prayer in expectant faith for that coming to greater conscious awareness of the presence and power of the Holy Spirit that charismatics term "the baptism in the Spirit."

   Priests should consider the humbling experience of asking the people in their prayer group to lay hands on them and ask for them to do this. If this is too difficult or threatening, the priest may ask some fellow priests who have had this experience to pray for him.

6. Priests grappling with problems such as authority in the Church, personal celibacy, or priestly identity can be helped much by the renewal. However, they should refuse a leadership role until they have reached a certain inner equilibrium or until such time as other people, mature in the Spirit, judge advisable.

7. Pastors have a special role toward a prayer group in their parish and should exercise the same type of leadership toward it as toward any other group in the parish. This includes a special role of discerning the fruits of the group. However pastors should not assume leadership in the inner workings of a prayer group except in line with what was expressed above.

8. A charismatic prayer group should not be "an organization we want in our parish" and which is started without much prayer or discernment. Its inception and growth should take place in a context of personal and communal prayer joined with consultation of others, laymen and/or priests, who are experienced in the renewal. The important thing is that "the Lord build the house; otherwise they labor in vain who build it" (Ps. 127).

9. A priest in a leadership role should seek to discern all the gifts and ministries in the group (as well as in his parish at large). He should call forth the exercise of these gifts and ministries and be ready to share his role with others who have leadership gifts. The Spirit

seldom gives all leadership gifts to the same person, at least not all in the same intensity, and wants a collegial dimension even at this grass roots level of Church life.

10. There are two extremes priests should be careful to avoid:

a) Downplaying the role of charismatic gifts. This attitude could be expressed: "We have a good group here, people are praying more and have a deeper faith. Let's keep this new depth and settle back to things as normal."

Vatican II in its documents on the Church and on the Apostolate of the Laity stressed that the Holy Spirit sanctifies his people not only through the hierarchy and sacraments but also through the charismatic gifts. The Spirit's presence is made manifest by these charismatic gifts and ministries. Today he is giving his church an abundance of these gifts to call us back to the Lord Jesus in repentance and more total commitment, and to himself in full openness. To deemphasize the gifts and ministries of the Spirit in their full spectrum is to deemphasize the tools he is using to renew the Church.

b) Overplaying one's own gifts or supposed gifts. Some people, both laymen and priests, compensate for their own insecurities and sense of unimportance by becoming *somebody* through the exercise of a spiritual gift. Examples are prophecy and healing.

Sometimes the person does not possess the gift at all. Sometimes it is present but the person uses it in such a way that it does not contribute to the glory of the Lord Jesus and the building up of his body, the Church.

The works of the flesh and fruit of the Spirit listed in Galatians 5:16-26 are good criteria by which to judge the authenticity and right use of a gift.

11. One of the most life-giving gifts to the People of God is a Christ-like priest serving according to his gifts. The charismatic renewal needs an abundance of such priests and already has a growing number of them.

The active presence of priests in the renewal is a necessity. But let them be humble men, men of prayer and men willing to work within the context, not of their preconceived notions, but of he whose thoughts are not our thoughts and whose ways are not our ways. A willingness to accept the discernment of people experienced in the renewal and ultimately of their bishop is the best sign that priests are proceeding in the wisdom of the Holy Spirit.

6

Parish Life Renewed
in the Power of the Spirit

It is very difficult to describe how a renewed parish will
look. The difficulty arises in part from the vast differences
which exist among parishes, and in part because we are
only starting to see parish renewal in the power of the
Spirit.

This chapter is a tentative attempt to describe some of
the ways the charismatic renewal can bring a renewal to
the life of the parish. The description will focus on what
the charismatic renewal can offer the parish. We will
examine the broad vision of parishes renewed in the
power of the Spirit primarily by discussing how elements
of the charismatic renewal can contribute to this vision.

Only some of these contributions involve the introduction of charismatic gifts and expressive praise into parish
life. These are important contributions, but many other
aspects of the charismatic renewal can make a contribution to parish renewal. In particular, some of the guiding

principles employed to build up the charismatic renewal are universal principles for building up any body of Christians, and should belong to the whole life of the Church.

For example, the practical advice Bert Ghezzi offers to prayer groups in his book *Build With The Lord* are not only matters of concern to prayer groups. Ghezzi discusses ways to develop leaders teams, develop effective worship, introduce others into a fuller life in the Spirit, provide teaching to foster growth in the Christian life, and establish loving relationships among Christians. These are matters of concern to every parish. Parishes renewing and changing these areas of their lives can profitably draw on the charismatic renewal's experience.

The greatest contribution that the charismatic renewal can make to the renewal of parish life is personally renewed Christians. The health and well-being of the Body of Christ depends on the health of its individual members. Parish renewal cannot be accomplished except through the renewal of individual Christian lives. Since the Church is an ordered community of people in relationship with God and with each other, the spiritual well-being of each individual has an effect on the whole.

We sometimes neglect this central fact and tend to think about parish renewal in terms of updating traditional practices, changing structures, and adopting new patterns of life. Such changes are sometimes necessary and important. But there is also a limit to the extent of genuine renewal such things can bring.

To draw an analogy, a family could move to a different city, buy a new house and new furniture, and become involved in many new activities. But such changes would leave the basics of family life untouched. The quality of the family's life would still depend on how the members of the family relate to each other, how loving and self-sacrificing each person is, how the children are growing to maturity, and how the husband and wife lay down their lives for each other and for their children.

Similarly, a parish could change many elements of its life—and find that not much had really changed. This in fact has been the common experience of the Church in years after Vatican II. Parish councils have been a step forward for the Church—but they have generally accomplished a lot less than they were expected to. Changes in the liturgy have been helpful—but many parishioners still have a difficult time praying. Much debate is currently raging over the issue of Communion in the hand—but the outcome will not make a significant difference in the lives of most Catholics.

Much of the hope for Church renewal awakened by the Second Vatican Council has now been lost. It has dissipated in part because too much emphasis was placed on structural renewal to the neglect of a deeper spiritual renewal. Without a renewal of people's lives, the Church found itself about the same that it had always been —except for being slightly confused and disillusioned that the anticipated renewal had not occurred.

While the charismatic renewal may assist in changing some structural elements of parish life, its most important contribution is personal spiritual renewal. The charismatic renewal can offer the Church parishioners who have come alive spiritually, and who can become dynamic participants in parish life.

This observation may disappoint those charismatics who visualize parish renewal along more structural lines.

They see a renewed parish as one where the charismatic gifts flourish during the celebration of Sunday liturgy, where most parishioners pray in tongues with arms upraised, where the prayer group leaders have been elected to the parish council. Some of these visible and structural changes may be good things to happen, but they are still means to an end, not the end itself.

The goal of parish renewal and charismatic renewal is a fully functioning body of Christ, composed of Christians whose lives are flourishing in their relationship with God, in their relations with one another, and in the growth of the fruits of the Spirit. A charismatically renewed parish will primarily manifest the presence and love of Jesus; only secondarily will it manifest specifically "charismatic" elements. It is more important that people pray than that they pray in tongues; it is more important that people love each other at the Sunday liturgy than that they exercise spiritual gifts; it is more important that members of the parish draw closer to each other in Christ than that they become involved in the charismatic renewal.

Charismatic gifts have an important role to play, but their role must be seen in proper perspective. The Lord gives gifts to build up the Body of Christ. Since the Body of Christ is made up of people in relationship to the Father and each other through Christ, the key to renewal is in renewed Christian lives.

The charismatic renewal is speaking a prophetic word to the Church today: lives need to be transformed by the power of the Holy Spirit. Most Catholics need to experience the salvation of Jesus Christ more explicitly; most need to experience the presence of the Holy Spirit in their lives more fully. The charismatic renewal has been successful precisely because it has focused on these fundamental realities. It has been effective in leading people to a deeper commitment to Christ and to a release of the power of the Spirit in their lives.

Consequently, the gifts of the Spirit are of importance to parish renewal. The specific practices and forms of piety employed by the charismatic renewal may be only means to growth in the Christian life, but they should not be deemphasized as "merely" means to a more significant end. St. Paul said that the greatest work of the Spirit was love, but he did not say that prophecy was unimportant, or that Christians should despise any of the gifts of the Spirit. He said the opposite: we should seek the gifts of the Spirit as means of building up the Body of Christ in love. Similarly, the approaches taken by the charismatic renewal today should be evaluated in light of their effectiveness in leading to a transformation of people's lives in Jesus Christ.

The charismatic renewal does not bestow instant sanctity or maturity. It cannot supply the Church with a group of people who are completely selfless in their love, mature in their judgment, and unstinting in their service of the parish. However, the charismatic renewal should be able to provide the parish with a group of people whose lives have been changed, who have experienced something of the love of God and the power of the Holy Spirit, and who are on the path to spiritual maturity. Through their involvement in the charismatic renewal, Christians normally find a renewed dedication to God and much eagerness to serve him.

The infusion into the parish of men and women who have experienced an awakening or reawakening in their spiritual lives should make a significant difference in itself. Even if nothing else in the parish changes, the presence and involvement of spiritually renewed Catholics should bring an important dimension of renewal to the parish.

Spiritually renewed parishioners should be able to make a difference simply by bringing a new vigor, joy, and enthusiasm to parish life. Parish life today often seems weak not because of what is done, but how it is done. If a Sunday liturgy seems "dead," it is not because the prayers and readings are incorrect, but because the congregation does not convey the impression that it is truly involved in what is happening. A hymn is "dead" when the congregation sings it half-heartedly; the same hymn sung wholeheartedly in praise of the Father seems to take on a new dimension. While prayer cannot be evaluated solely in terms of exterior signs, the responsiveness of a community at prayer is significant. In most parishes, it is the congregation's responsiveness, not the liturgy, which is most in need of renewal.

We can make the same point about many parish activities. For example, a parish may have a St. Vincent de Paul Society with a small and overworked group of men carrying out various works of mercy. What the society often needs most is not a new structure, but more willing steady workers, and more people in the parish who will come forth when the need arises.

Pastors and active laypeople are painfully aware of the many works and services in every parish that go unperformed because no one steps forth (or can be dragged forth) to undertake them. People involved in the charismatic renewal can often help, for one of the changes that usually occurs in their lives is a much greater generosity and self-confidence in undertaking roles of service. Involvement, not passivity, is the norm in the charismatic renewal; it should also be the norm for parish life.

Another area of parish life that can flourish simply through the involvement of spiritually renewed parishioners is the often disappointing quality of Christian fellowship. Sometimes parishes are too large for fellowship to happen easily, but even where parishes have been broken into smaller geographic areas to encourage close contact among parishioners, the results are often decidedly mixed. Sometimes priests have offered to say home masses for small gatherings of parishioners from one neighborhood—and have been greeted with apathy. If parishioners simply made an effort to get to know their Catholic neighbors and to serve them, the level of Christian fellowship in a parish would increase dramatically. In short, no new organization or structure can overcome parishioners' disinterest in each other. If, on the other hand, such basic interest and commitment are present, finding suitable structures for its expression should not be a difficult task.

Indeed, if nothing changed in our parishes except the commitment and enthusiasm with which things were done, parishes would begin to experience a renewed life. It is on this level that the charismatic renewal has its first contribution to make. By supplying parishioners whose lives are in the process of being renewed, the charismatic renewal can provide the basis for parish renewal. The foundation of parish renewal consists of parishioners who have experienced the love of God in a personal way, who focus their lives on the Lordship of Jesus Christ, who are open to the working of the Holy Spirit in their lives, and who have a desire to enter into deeper Christian fellowship. These are the men and women who will be among those who enter wholeheartedly into the worship of the liturgy, who will form bonds of personal relationships with other parishioners, and who will expend their lives in serving others.

While renewed individuals are the foundation for parish renewal, there are areas of parish life that do need to be changed in order for a parish to fully carry out its mission. The following is a brief discussion of how the charismatic renewal has experience and insight to offer in some specific areas of parish renewal.

Shared ministry. Despite much discussion of "collegiality" and "coresponsibility" after Vatican II, most parishes still display a rather sharp distinction between the active ministry of the priests and the passive participation of the vast majority of the laity. While a handful of laypeople may help the pastor in various works of the parish, and while parish councils may have involved the laity in decision-making, most of the pastoral work of the parish is still carried on by its priests.

In most parishes, contact between priest and people is largely limited to liturgical functions. Most parishes are adequately staffed with priests to perform these liturgical functions and care for the basic administration of the parish. However, the other pastoral functions of the parish are generally intermittent and involve relatively small numbers of parishioners. In particular, most parishioners do not receive effective individual attention in helping them grow in the Christian life. If the pastor and his assistants tried to provide this care on a large scale, they would soon reach their limit of time and energy.

The charismatic renewal has two things to offer the parish in this regard: an awareness of the variety of ministry gifts and roles, and an increased number of pastoral leaders.

Most prayer groups of any size and maturity have discovered that a pastoral team of leaders is necessary to meet their needs. No one "charismatic leader" has either the gifts or the time to fulfill all the necessary leadership functions. Instead, team leadership has emerged: a group of people who have made a commitment to the group and to each other to serve the group as leaders. Each member of the pastoral team contributes his own gifts and abilities—and, most importantly, himself—to caring for the needs of the group. In a mature leaders team, a genuine "shared ministry" develops, where the burdens of pastoral leadership fall on no one person, but upon the team as a whole.

The church has recognized the benefits of shared leadership, and has been making various efforts at "team ministry," some of them involving religious and laity along with priests. However, the burden of pastoral care for a parish usually still rests with the pastor and other ordained clergy. The charismatic renewal can bring to the Church an increasing amount of experience in how a more coresponsible style of leadership may be exercised. This will not undermine the pastor and his authority; it does mean that the pastor will exercise his role and his authority in a different way. Shared ministry means that the core of every parish will be found less in one man, and more in a group of people, led by the pastor, providing overall pastoral leadership and service to the parish.

Shared ministry naturally requires more pastorally skilled people in the parish. Here too the charismatic renewal has something to offer. When the charismatic renewal first began, leadership was pretty much limited to overseeing what went on during the prayer meetings. Through often painful experience, it was learned that much more extensive leadership was needed. If people were to grow to maturity in the life of the Spirit, what went on in people's lives between prayer meetings was more important than the meetings themselves. Gradually many groups shifted their focus from simply providing leadership for a prayer meeting to providing leadership for a prayer group—a group of people.

The style and extent of prayer group leadership varies greatly and is still evolving, but there is a trend toward prayer group leaders serving people in their whole lives, not merely in their prayer lives. This role does not involve asserting authority over people against their wishes, but it does frequently involve a variety of pastoral functions and services going far beyond running an orderly prayer meeting. An increasing number of leaders are becoming experienced in providing pastoral help for people through the charismatic renewal. They will become an increasingly valuable resource for the Church as ways are found for the parish to draw upon their experience and skills.

In a charismatically renewed parish, it is not hard to imagine pastoral leadership and service being provided by a pastoral team under the leadership of the pastor, instead of by a pastor struggling to carry the burden by himself. The team would possess the wide variety of gifts of service necessary for the parish: gifts of teaching, planning, counseling, administration, discernment, healing, and other functions needed for the well-being of the parish. The pastoral team together would keep the parish as a whole as its concern, and seek the Lord for overall direction. Each member would serve as his particular gifts enabled him to. The team would be headed by the pastor, who would retain final overall authority. But it would operate as a pastoral team, sharing the work of serving the parish.

Shared ministry must extend beyond the pastoral team to include every parishioner in his appropriate role of service. Every Christian is called and gifted by the Holy Spirit for service in the Body of Christ, and every parishioner should be sharing in the mission and ministry of the parish. Not every role of service will be highly visible, but a renewed parish will be characterized by widespread active involvement in service and ministry. There should be no completely "passive" parishioner. The weakness of many parishes today stems precisely from the passivity of parishioners, and their low level of involvement in worthwhile service.

Guidance. The importance of receiving God's guidance in knowing how to integrate the charismatic renewal into the life of the parish was discussed in Chapter 4. The same principles apply to the parish as a whole. Receiving the guidance of the Holy Spirit is necessary for any assembly of Christians, and is crucial for parishes today.

Most parish councils approach problems and arrive at decisions by a process little different from that used by any group of decision-makers. Their deliberations involve discussion, debate, and an occasional argument. The matter is resolved by a vote, or by an exercise of the pastor's veto. Typically, the council seeks no specifically Christian wisdom to apply to the discussion. It employs no means of listening to the Lord to hear his specific guidance.

Catholic charismatics have no secret channel to God. Yet the charismatic renewal does have some experience to offer the Church about seeking God's will and discerning the right course of action. The basic elements of seeking guidance discussed in Chapter 4 need to be employed by any group of Christians faced with important decisions.

A parish renewed in the power of the Spirit would continually make a conscious effort to seek God's will in matters of major importance. Parish councils and other decision-making bodies would discuss, debate, and weigh all the alternatives. But they would also pray for guidance, they would be open to receiving direction through prophecy, and they would discern and test the various leadings that were received. The overall atmosphere of decision-making would be characterized by prayer rather than by debate; there would be an effort to achieve oneness of mind and heart rather than a compromise and a balance of power.

The pastor should lead the parish in seeking the will of God in matters of major direction and importance. The parish council should be an integral part of this process. The parish as a whole should have a sense of involvement: the parish should greet a decision with the feeling "This is what *we* decided," not "This is what *they* decided."

There should be a sense that "This is what the Lord told *us,*" not "This is what the Lord apparently told *them.*"

Effective evangelism. The Church's evangelistic outreach has shown unmistakable signs of decreasing vitality. The number of converts to the Catholic Church has declined steadily for a number of years. An increased ecumenical sensitivity to Protestant Christians cannot account for this, for about half of the population of the United States has no church membership, and clearly stands in need of hearing the message of the gospel. Because Chrsitianity by its very nature is a faith that must be proclaimed, an effective parish must exercise an effective evangelical outreach.

To some degree, the charismatic renewal has proven that it can effectively bring the good news about Jesus Christ to others. It has done so not so much through evangelism campaigns as through helping Catholics come alive in their Christian lives to a noticeable degree. Others respond more readily to the gospel when it is accompanied by the witness of lives changed through the power of the Spirit. A parish renewed in the power of the Spirit should be a community of changed and changing lives.

However, we must not neglect another dimension to evangelism. The aim of evangelism is to incorporate individuals into the Body of Christ. Converts must be incorporated into a body of Christians and become a part of its life if evangelism is to yield significant and long-lasting results. The early Church practiced this approach. Conversion was seen as a process of repentance and instruction, culminating in baptism during the Easter vigil. A new convert was systematically prepared for baptism by means of a "catechumenate." This catechumenate involved a time of experiencing the life of the Church as much as it was a time of formal instruction.

The charismatic renewal is developing a sort of catechumenate as well. Experience has shown that it is not enough to simply pray over people and get them baptized in the Holy Spirit. A time of preparation and instruction is necessary—such as that provided by the *Life in the Spirit Seminars*. The overwhelming acceptance and widespread use of the *Life in the Spirit Seminars* indicates that this program is highly effective in helping people find a new or renewed Christian life.

Parishes need something like the *Life in the Spirit Seminars* to initiate converts into the Christian life and bring renewal to the lives of long-time Catholics. Most parish convert inquiry classes go only part of the way. They provide an instructional introduction to Catholicism, but do not give converts an experiential introduction into the Christian life and bring them into living relationships with other Christians—the needs that were met by the early Church's catechumenate. Most parishes also lack an effective means of helping their current members experience a rejuvenation of their Christian lives. At one time, retreats met such a need, but they seem to have declined in their popularity.

Some parishes might be able to simply adopt the *Life in the Spirit Seminars* as a regular parish program, making it a part of their process of initiating converts into the Church and also offering it to all parishioners as a means of personal renewal. However, this should be done with caution, and only if the pastor thoroughly understands the *Life in the Spirit Seminars* and wants to use them this way.

In other cases, parishes might adapt and modify the seminars, tailoring them to their particular needs and the openness of the parish to the charismatic renewal.

However the parish approaches it, the basic problem is that the effective parish needs a means of initiating converts into its life and renewing the Christian lives of its members. The charismatic renewal has found an effective means of accomplishing very similar aims in the *Life in the Spirit Seminars*. The seminars, or a very similar program, should be a part of the pastoral strategy of every parish seeking renewal in the power of the Spirit.

Teaching for growth. The increased emphasis on adult education in the Church since the Second Vatican Council is an important trend. The continuing formation of adults is necessary, not simply to keep Catholics abreast of changes in the Church, but more basically because the Christian life by its nature calls for continuing growth into the image of Christ. Catechetical instruction for children, long the Church's primary educational task, is insufficient to form a mature adult faith. Adult faith requires adult instruction.

Unfortunately, most Catholic adults seem uninterested in adult education programs. Most parish programs of adult education attract only a few percent of the parishioners—occasionally more, sometimes even less. Priests and educators may bemoan this state of affairs —but no one has found a way to remedy it.

However, those involved in the charismatic renewal are an encouraging exception to this overall picture. These men and women are generally very eager to receive ongoing instruction on how to grow in the Christian life.

They seem to recognize that spiritual experience, the *Life in the Spirit Seminars,* and attendance at prayer meetings are not enough to lead them to full maturity in the Christian life. Consequently, they seek out courses of instruction, workshops which share the practical wisdom of others, and books and tapes which contain helpful teaching. The rapid growth of *New Covenant* magazine—a magazine which is oriented toward teaching which can help its readers mature in their Christian commitment—is an index of the hunger that exists in the charismatic renewal for ongoing teaching. The demand for packaged "foundation" courses covering basic aspects of the Christian life is another index of such craving.

This hunger of charismatic Catholics for continuing religious education has obvious implications for the renewal of parish adult education programs. The *Life in the Spirit Seminars,* foundations courses, and other teaching programs developed in the charismatic renewal can infuse an effective new approach into existing adult religious education programs. At the same time, Catholic charismatics seeking more teaching for growth should increase the demand for these programs.

The Church can learn something from the charismatic renewal about how to develop effective adult formation programs. Many parish programs are already excellent, but others are too theoretical, lacking the practical focus that people are hungry for. Theologically oriented programs are important, but there is also a largely unmet need for practical Christian wisdom about persistent problems and basic needs in the Christian life. Formation programs are needed to deal with such questions as "How can I love God more? How should I go about praying and reading

Scripture? How can I bring up my children as Christians? How can I know what God's will is for me? How can I overcome my persistent temptations? What is my proper role of service to others? How does my job fit into God's plan for my life? How can our marriage grow stronger?''

The charismatic renewal can offer many parishes practical teaching dealing with such questions as these. Of course, the charismatic renewal has no monopoly on wisdom about these matters. But a parish seeking renewal in the power of the Spirit should draw upon whatever resources it can—including the basic Christian teaching which is developing in the charismatic renewal.

Worship. Liturgical renewal has rightly been a focus of parish renewal for many years. Worship must be at the center of the life of every parish. The Second Vatican Council declared that ''the liturgy is the summit toward which the activity of the Church is directed; at the same time it is the fountain from which all her power flows.'' While this is a theologically correct statement, it hardly describes the actual experience of many parishes in their life of worship together. Despite the great efforts in liturgical renewal since the Council, far too many Catholics still sit passively through Sunday mass, apparently neither greatly infused with the power of God nor profoundly worshipping him.

In contrast, a parish renewed in the power of the Spirit should manifest a reverent enthusiasm during its gatherings for liturgical celebration. Mass should seem ''alive.'' If the Sunday liturgy is theologically the high point of the parish's week, it should also be the high point of the weekly lives of its parishioners.

The charismatic renewal is quite successful in fostering a renewed sense of worship. Most prayer meetings are characterized by wholehearted worship. These gatherings are usually marked by both joyful enthusiasm and profound and solemn worship. Even a casual visitor can sense that the Lord is present and that his people are worshipping him. This manifest sense of worship is perhaps the most effective means of evangelism and growth for prayer groups: as people come in contact with wholehearted prayer, they are drawn to take part in it.

The continued renewal of the liturgical life of a parish can only take place as parishioners grow in their capability to participate and worship. Partly this will be the result of individually renewed lives. Partly this will be the result of conscious preparation before attending the liturgy, to prepare ourselves to enter into worship and celebration. Partly this will result from adopting new forms of praise and worship, in keeping with the true nature of the Eucharistic sacrifice.

Simply assuming "pentecostal" styles of worship into the liturgy will not accomplish a renewal of the liturgy. In many cases, attempts to "pentecostalize" the mass will only create severe divisions within the parish. In liturgical renewal, perhaps more than any other aspect of parish life, the pastor's role of discerning and directing is indispensable.

Yet the charismatic renewal does contain elements which in the years to come should become a part of the liturgical life of the parish. The charismatic gifts which are normally used during prayer meetings are not merely gifts for prayer meetings. They are gifts for the Church, and should find a place in the normal life of the Church.

Some prayer groups, operating under the guidance of the pastor, regularly celebrate a mass which includes the use of the spiritual gifts. These groups are gaining wisdom about the proper role of prophecy during the liturgy, about the appropriate use of spontaneous praise, and about the value of times of silent adoration. Their experience should be useful for the whole Church.

Parishes should proceed with discernment and caution as they integrate charismatic elements into the liturgy. A prophecy proclaimed to an assembly which does not accept prophecy as a valid gift cannot function as God's word to that assembly; singing in tongues in the midst of a congregation which does not accept the validity of prayer in tongues can only cause division. As the one presiding over the public worship of the parish, the pastor must discern what is appropriate at any given time for that parish. Perhaps a special "charismatic mass" on Sunday would be an effective way to begin introducing charismatic elements into the parish's worship. Perhaps the use of spiritual gifts must be restricted to more private gatherings until the parish has received more instruction and is able to accept the use of spiritual gifts in the liturgy.

Unity. One of the characteristics of a parish renewed in the power of the Spirit will be its unity. Chapter 2 discusses how the charismatic renewal can be a point of division within a parish. Here, paradoxical as it may seem, we shall discuss how the charismatic renewal is called to bring a new depth of unity to parish life.

Most Catholic parishes are not known for their unity. Usually a surface peace prevails, but often serious divisions lie beneath. Sometimes the divisions break out into the open, particularly when the parish faces some major decision. The points of contention can be many: those who favor more rapid change in the Church oppose those who are comfortable with little or no change; those who wish to improve religious education classes find themselves divided from those who support the Catholic school; those who want to sing loudly at mass bother those who want to pray in silence.

While the charismatic renewal in some places has become a point of division, it also has succeeded in creating unity where none before existed. In the charismatic renewal, liberals and conservatives, Catholics and Protestants, young and old find unity in their common experience of the reality and presence of God. Broken friendships have been healed, estranged families reunited, and those who would never have even spoken to each other before now find themselves united in heart. To be sure, internal disunity within prayer groups sometimes happens. However, the more characteristic experience is that the charismatic renewal brings unity in areas where none existed before.

This unity has been chiefly an *internal* unity: a unity among those who participate in the charismatic renewal. The division over the movement has often been an *external* division: those in the charismatic renewal are sometimes divided from those who are not.

If the charismatic renewal is called to bring increased unity to parish life, it will do so by focusing on two bedrocks of unity: our common salvation in Jesus Christ, and our call to pursue unending reconciliation with our brothers.

St. Paul is quite clear about the source of unity among Christians: it is our baptism into one Christ. Nothing else that we might share in common can provide the fundamental basis of our unity. And contrariwise, nothing that might divide us should divide us if we are united in our life in Christ. Our unity cannot be based on having had similar spiritual experiences, or praying in the same style. Our unity must be based on Christ. Similarly, we cannot consider ourselves divided from other Christians because they have not had our spiritual experiences, do not speak our jargon, or prefer a different style of prayer. What Christ has united, we cannot sunder by our minor differences.

This is a word of unity that must be spoken to the Church. If the charismatic renewal is to speak the word, it must speak it humbly—for the charismatic renewal itself still needs to repair disunity in its midst, and disunity between it and the parish. But the message of our unity in Christ must be proclaimed. More importantly, it must be lived.

The charismatic renewal has also developed some wisdom in repairing unity once it has been broken. The groups which have accumulated the most extensive experience in this area are those which have developed into Christian communities with Christians of many different temperaments joining together in close fellowship. A commitment to brotherhood in community does not mean that misunderstandings and problems will not arise. Rather, it means that Christians have a commitment to work differences out in Christ and to continually pursue reconciliation until it is achieved.

Much of this experience in reconciliation is useful for parishes. A parish renewed in the power of the Spirit will not be a parish where everyone agrees with each other, or even necessarily naturally likes each other. However, a renewed parish will be a place where members are committed to seeking reconciliation as soon as unity has been broken. Such a parish will offer regular teaching on reconciliation, and continually practice reconciliation through the Sacrament of Penance and other means. It will be a parish united in at least one regard: all parishioners are committed to overcome all disunity.

Community. Theologically, a parish is the most local manifestation of the Body of Christ—a community of believers who have found salvation in Jesus Christ. However, most Catholic parishes can be called communities only in the loosest sense of that word. Anonymity pervades parish life: we often do not know the person who worships next to us in the pew during Sunday mass. Sometimes this anonymity is the result of the sheer size of large parishes. But too often, parishioners do not know each other because they do not seem to be very interested in forming closer ties with other Christians.

Community is not the result of making a specified number of changes in parish life or adopting certain structures. At its root, Christian community is based upon the personal commitment of Christians to each other. Certain structures can facilitate the development of community—but only if the basic ingredient of commitment is present.

The evolution of some charismatic prayer groups into communities has followed this path: they have developed as their members have grown in their commitment to one another. Community will grow in parishes in no other way. The foundation of community is the commitment of lives laid down for one another in Christ.

At the same time, pastoral leaders can take practical steps to call forth and facilitate this commitment. Preaching in the parish should call people on in fellowship and brotherhood. Opportunities must be created for people to get to know one another and to serve one another. Many large parishes could well be restructured into smaller units. Sharing groups and ongoing Scripture study groups may help meet needs for fellowship. A well-celebrated liturgy should help create a sense of community, a sense that everyone is a part of a living unity of the Body of Christ.

In essence, a parish is made up of people in relationship with one another. If the relationships are distant and formal, the parish will show few of the visible signs of Christian community. If the relationships are personal and loving, the parish will be on the road to being a community in fact as well as in theory. If the relationships are ones of deep commitment to each other in Christ, then a foundation will exist for full community life. A parish renewed in the power of the Spirit will be a parish where the relationships among parishioners have been transformed, where parishioners are committed to laying down their lives for one another, where the love of parishioners for each other occupies a primary place in their lives. The example of successful charismatic groups in achieving community should be a stimulus to parishes, and a source of practical wisdom.

Help when it is needed. Most prayer groups find that a good many people with various personal needs are attracted to them. Some of these people come because they need to be noticed, esteemed, and loved. Some come for help with difficult family problems. Some come with even deeper problems and troubles. Behind the middle-class facade of American society are many people in need, people who are lonely, people who are overlooked, people who have trouble living a normal and fulfilling life.

While prayer groups generally find that they cannot give all the help that is needed, most of them can give many people some help, often invaluable help. This is not "professional" help by any means; it is mostly the help of people who are willing to open up their lives to others, who are willing to do whatever they can to help and console others, who are always willing to pray with and for others.

Any Christian community should be a place where those in need can come for acceptance and help. Parishes should have the capability of providing such support and help, but too often parishes are heavier in the institutional and administrative side of their lives than the personal and community side. Often the rectory is the only place that people in need can go for help, and overworked priests find their resources limited.

A parish renewed in the power of the Spirit should be a place of refuge and help. It should be a place where people can find affirmation and healing. It should be a place where broken people find access to the power of the Spirit to mend their lives. Charismatic groups are meant to bring their own experience in healing lives to the parish—and to be a body of people within the parish who are willing to open their lives to those in need.

Spiritual power. Catholic parishes sometimes seem to be unable to make much difference in the world today. While everything that is done in the parish might be proper and orthodox, its impact on its parishioners and on its neighborhood often seems quite limited. The gospel is preached accurately—but conversion and spiritual growth do not seem to result. The parish is operated efficiently—but lives do not seem to be changed. At the end of a year, parish life seems as it was when the year began. Something seems to be missing.

By contrast, the early Christians seemed to have a far greater spiritual vitality. The early Church could draw upon a power far greater than mere human effort when it invited people to faith in Jesus Christ and called them to maturity in that faith. When the Church took root in a city, that city knew about it. When the gospel was proclaimed, hearts were changed. When men joined the Church, their lives were changed. This did not happen because the apostles were highly skilled organizers, brilliant preachers, or extra diligent workers. It happened because the power of the Spirit was at work in their midst.

The Church today stands in need of a renewed power of the Spirit in its midst. It needs to be able to demonstrate the presence and power of the Spirit both to its own members and to the world. It needs to be a more effective sign of God's presence among his people. It needs to be able to proclaim the gospel, not with mere human eloquence, but with "a demonstration of the power of the Spirit'' (1 Cor. 2:5). It needs to be able to bring a healing to broken lives on a more fundamental level than welfare agencies and social workers can do. It needs to be able to say "I give you what I have: in the name of Jesus Christ the Nazarene, walk!" (Acts 3:6).

The charismatic renewal is precisely a renewal in the power of the Holy Spirit. It does not owe its success to mastery of sophisticated organizational theory or to an effective use of modern communications. The charismatic renewal is successful because people experience the power of the Holy Spirit through it, and their lives are changed. They find nourishment for their spiritual hunger, healing for their minds and bodies, and an experience of the presence and power of God.

If there is any key to the charismatic renewal's experience of this power of God, it is simply the key of faith. Catholic charismatics are certainly no more intelligent or holy than other Catholics. If anything distinguishes them, it is simply their recognition that they need the power of God in their lives and their expectant faith that they will receive it. If charismatics seem to receive more from God, it is simply because they ask more.

The charismatic renewal can help the Church find renewal in the power of the Spirit. This will happen when the parish is permeated by an expectant faith that calls upon and relies upon the power of the Holy Spirit. This should be one result of the integration of the charismatic renewal into the life of the parish, and a foundation for renewal in the power of the Spirit.

The charismatic renewal does not have *the* answer for every area of renewal discussed in this chapter. In most of these areas, the charismatic renewal itself has much to learn and implement. These areas of parish renewal should rather be viewed as challenges for both the parish and the charismatic renewal. They are areas where the charismatic renewal can make a contribution. They are also challenges which, when met, reveal something of the nature of the life of a parish renewed in the power of the Holy Spirit.

A parish renewed in the power of the Spirit will above all be a parish made up of men and women who have personally given their lives over to the Lordship of Jesus and experienced the power of the Spirit in their lives. It will be a parish in living contact with God. It will be a parish led by a pastor presiding over a pastoral team exercising shared ministry, seeking the guidance of the Holy Spirit, and developing effective programs for evangelism, initiation into the Christian life, and continued growth into Christian maturity. It will be a parish centered on worship of the Lord. It will be a parish whose members are committed to each other and to achieving ever-fuller unity. It will be a parish that manifests the power of the Spirit.

7

Being a Servant

When we compare the grand goals of integrating the charismatic renewal into parish life and renewing the parish in the power of the Spirit with the realities of our own parish and prayer group, the contrast can be very sobering. Few parishes strike us as dynamic Christian communities. Many pastors are uncertain about what to do with the charismatic renewal. Many prayer groups are struggling, and many prayer group leaders are unsure of themselves. The charismatic renewal of parish life can seem to be a long way off.

The renewal of the Church and the absorption of the charismatic movement into the life of the Church will happen neither quickly nor automatically. Nor will it happen except by the sovereign grace of God. The Church will always stand in need of renewal. It is made up of individuals who will always stand in need of forgiveness from sin and of further growth in the Christian life. The Church will be a ''finished product'' only when Jesus completes the work of redeeming his body by his coming again.

In the meantime, we can be prey to a number of temptations. We can be tempted to believe that we have undertaken an impossible task: our parish will never experience renewal in the power of the Spirit, our efforts to integrate the charismatic movement into parish life are fruitless. We can start thinking of ourselves as "voices crying out in the wilderness"—voices whose message of good news is unwelcomed and unheeded. We can be tempted to two deadly and related sins: discouragement and pride. Either of them can quench the work of the Spirit in our parish.

The temptation to discouragement is natural. Our parish can seem to be a vast immovable institution, complex in its makeup, entrenched in its ways, uninterested in true renewal. Our prayer group can appear to us to be hopelessly on the fringe of parish life, ignored by most of the parishioners or looked upon with amusement. Even if the pastor is sympathetic, his many responsibilities may prevent him from devoting the time to the charismatic renewal that we would hope for. Our initial hopes for a rapid transformation of parish life may now strike us as totally unrealistic, and we wonder if there is any hope for real progress.

In the face of temptations to discouragement, it is well to reflect that peace and patience are listed among the fruits of the Spirit. We are called to have an underlying peace in whatever situation we are in. Not that we are to be content with the way things are: many situations need to be changed, and they need our prayer and action for change to come about. But we are called to be peaceful about our place in God's plan and trust his timing as he unfolds his plan. We are called to be peaceful because God loves us despite whatever situation we are in. The follower of Jesus should experience his peace as he becomes fully involved in the often hard work of bringing his kingdom to come on earth.

God demonstrated extraordinary patience in unfolding his plan of salvation for man. Many centuries passed between the appearance of man upon the earth and the call of Abraham. Centuries passed between the first covenant, given through Moses, and the new covenant, given in Jesus Christ. Even in the life of Jesus we see a divine patience: many years of quiet life in Nazareth preceded the few years of public ministry. Jesus' followers were patient as well: about 10 years passed between Paul's conversion and his first missionary journey.

Our patience is often much more limited. We want a full renewal in the power of the Spirit for the Church, and we want it *now*. We tend to measure results in terms of weeks and months instead of decades and lifetimes. It *is* good to be eager about our Father's business—but only if our eagerness does not make us vulnerable to temptations to discouragement. Better than eagerness is steadfastness; better than enthusiasm is unwavering commitment. We need to set about the work we have been given with commitment; we need to be steadfastly faithful to it. Success depends on the sovereign grace of God, given in his good time, not ours.

As dangerous as discouragement is the temptation to pride. We have experienced new life through the charismatic renewal; in contrast to what we have experienced, the "normal" life of the Church seems dead. Our language often betrays us: we consider ourselves to be "Spirit-filled"—subtly implying that other Christians are not, or at least as not as completely as we are. If others do not welcome our initial attempts at bringing renewal in the power of the Spirit to our parish, we can be tempted to believe that our parish is simply closed to the action of the Lord in its midst.

In its severest form, pride can tempt us to forsake all efforts to serve and renew our parish. Why should we sacrifice ourselves to serve an institution that is "obviously" so lifeless? We can believe that ours is the only way God has for men to find salvation: if people in the parish want to experience new life, let them come to us. Of course, we rarely verbalize our pride this explicitly—but the aloofness born of pride isolates us just as effectively from parish life.

In its milder forms, pride gives rise to attitudes of superiority that can irritate and offend others. If our fellow parishioners detect a smugness, an elitism, or a messianic complex in our language and approach, it can isolate us from them. We may say we are "giving God the glory" for the great things he has done for us; others may detect only an attitude of pride in such remarks, and be irritated by it.

There is a need for the charismatic renewal to play a prophetic role in the Church today. The charismatic renewal is meant to contribute to the renewal of the Church, and to make a difference in the life of the Church and the life of the parish. But our basic approach to the Church should be less that of a prophet than that of a servant. There is a place for clear proclamation of the gospel; there are situations where a word of objective evaluation must be uttered; there may even be rare occasions when a ringing prophetic denunciation is called for. But the basic stance of the charismatic renewal toward the Church must be one of an obedient servant. The primary role of those involved in the charismatic renewal must be to serve, not to judge. When our fellow parishioners think of us, their first impression should be that charismatics are a people who love them and serve them, not a people who stand aloof and condemn them.

If we set our sights on reforming the Church, our patience and hope will be severely put to the test. If instead our aim is to serve, we should find it easier to be steadfast in our efforts and peaceful in our hope. If we hope for quick success in making a major impact we will most likely be disappointed, save for the sovereign grace of God. If instead we only ask an opportunity to love others on their terms, we will find that opportunity. If we champion our own cause too strongly, we will likely find ourselves in the midst of contention and division. If instead we approach the parish in humility, we will find an ever-growing unity with our fellow parishioners.

Our basic stance of being a servant must go deeper than a desire to "don't rock the boat" and "don't offend anyone." We must be a servant in imitation of Christ. If we desire unity in the body of Christ, if we desire renewal for the Church, if we desire to bring fuller life in Christ, then our own lives must be lived in imitation of Christ and our approach must be his approach.

This was St. Paul's exhortation to the Christians at Philippi. He urged them to seek complete unity: unity of purpose and convictions, unity of mind and heart. This unity was to be a flowering of what all Christians had in common: a common life in Christ, a common indwelling of the Holy Spirit, a common call to love. This unity could only be attained if there was no pride or competitiveness among Christians. Rather, Paul recommended just the opposite attitudes: everyone was to be self-effacing, considering the other person to be better than himself. This certainly leaves no room for prideful attitudes on the part of the "Spirit-filled" toward others. Instead, the focus must be on serving others: on thinking not of ourselves but of others; on not seeking our own advantage first, but seeking the advantage of others.

The attitudes and actions Paul recommends were not merely good human things to do. They were attitudes and actions done in imitation of Christ. Christ took human form in order to become the servant of his Father and the servant of man. His service was total, without reserve: he assumed the condition of slave for our sakes, even to the point of accepting the death of an outcast. But because of his lowly service, the Father raised him up—setting him on high as the one who must be worshipped and imitated. In our service, we are merely entering into this mystery.

If our life in Christ means anything to you, if love can persuade at all, or the Spirit that we have in common, or any tenderness and sympathy, then be united in your convictions and united in your love, with a common purpose and a common mind. That is the one thing which would make me completely happy. There must be no competition among you, no conceit; but everybody is to be self-effacing. Always consider the other person to be better than yourself, so that nobody thinks of his own interests first but everybody thinks of other people's interests instead. In your minds you must be the same as Christ Jesus: His state was divine, yet he did not cling to his equality with God but emptied himself to assume the condition of a slave, and became as all men are; and being as all men are, he was humbler yet, even to accepting death, death on a cross. But God raised him high and gave him the name which is above all other names so that all beings in the heaven, on earth and in the underworld should bend the knee at the name of Jesus and that every tongue should acclaim Jesus Christ as Lord, to the glory of God the Father.

(Phil. 2:1-11)